Dancing in the Rain
Words of comfort and hope for a sad heart

Dancing in the Rain: *Words of Comfort and Hope for a Sad Heart*

© Anusha Atukorala 2018

Published by Armour Books
P. O. Box 492, Corinda QLD 4075

Cover Photo: Canstock © Candy Box Images
Typeset by Book Whispers

ISBN: 978-1-925380-11-8

 A catalogue record for this book is available from the National Library of Australia

All rights reserved. No part of this publication may be reproduced, stored in, or introduced into a retrieval system, or transmitted, in any form, or by any means (electronic, mechanical, photocopying, recording or otherwise) without the prior written permission of the publisher.

Dancing in the Rain
Words of comfort and hope for a sad heart

Anusha Atukorala

Christopher Reeve quote, used by permission

Corrie Ten Boom quote, from Marching Orders for the End Battle, CLC Ministries, used by permission

Robert Brault quote, used by permission

Mary Anne Radmacher quote, from the poem courage, used by permission of the author

Frank Pittman quote, used by permission

C.S. Lewis quote, from The Problem of Pain by CS Lewis © copyright CS Lewis Pte Ltd 1940, used by permission

Viktor Frankl quote, from Logotherapy and the Challenge of Suffering, Beacon Press, used by permission

Scripture quotations marked ERV are taken from the HOLY BIBLE: EASY-TO-READ VERSION © 2001 by World Bible Translation Center, Inc. and used by permission.

Scripture quotations marked KJV are taken from the King James Version of the Bible. Public domain.

Scripture quotations marked NASB are taken from the New American Standard Bible®, Copyright © 1960, 1962, 1963, 1968, 1971, 1972, 1973, 1975, 1977, 1995 by The Lockman Foundation. Used by permission. (www.Lockman.org)

Scripture quotations marked NIV are taken from the HOLY BIBLE, NEW INTERNATIONAL VERSION®. Copyright © 1973, 1978, 1984 Biblica. Used by permission of Zondervan. All rights reserved.

Scripture quotations marked NKJV are taken from the New King James Version. Copyright © 1982 by Thomas Nelson, Inc. Used by permission. All rights reserved.

Scripture quotations marked MSG are taken from THE MESSAGE, copyright © 1993, 1994, 1995, 1996, 2000, 2001, 2002 by Eugene H. Peterson. Used by permission of NavPress. All rights reserved. Represented by Tyndale House Publishers, Inc.

Acknowledgments – Dancing in the Rain

Special thanks to special people …
- ***Shan***—my treasured husband of 32 years—you freed me to pursue my writing dreams while you worked long and hard to keep a roof over our heads and put bread on the table. Thank you too for your strong hand in mine when I've needed it, for being my dance partner through every season, many of them wet and soggy. *How can I thank you enough?* I love you very very much.
- ***Asela***—my son, my favourite son, my only son! Your perseverance and courage through life's challenges have taught me to keep dancing, even when the rain pelted down. You have prayed with me and for me; you have encouraged me. I'm so grateful to God for the gift of you.
- ***Amma and Thatha***—my cherished, precious, amazing parents. You gave me a stable, happy childhood which helped me stay strong when the storms raged. You placed my hand in God's—the best gift you could give. He strengthened me to face life's trials with joy, hope and courage. I'm so grateful to you and for you.
- ***Ashi***—my beloved daughter-niece, you've been the inspiration for this book. Thank you for loving me, for praying for me, for encouraging me and for being the unique, God-given daughter I never had. You are precious and dearly loved.
- ***Dileeni, Ranmali, Sal, Charmalie and Shiranthi,*** my unique

sisters and prayer partners in the Lord—your support and encouragement for more than forty years have inspired me, taught me and enriched my walk with God. I love you.
- *Melissa*—my beautiful God-given chum, I've shared many deep conversations, prayer sessions and writing dreams with you. You have blessed me my friend and I thank God for you.
- *My extended family,* you've been the backbone of my life for over 60 years.
  - My 6 brothers, *Ajit, Rohan, Ranjan, Dilip, Chandran & Ranil,*
  - My 6 sisters, *Ranmali, Swen, Niranji, Sharon, Sal & Charmalie,*
  - My nieces and nephews, *Indrajit & Sybil, Dhiren, Dil and Col, Ambrith and Sue, Allison, Alex and Lindsay, Chandri, Sheni and Pra, Ashi and Shala;* thank you for being a special part of my life.
  - My little grand-nieces and grand-nephews, *Kate, Rufus, Yannish, Rosie and Raya,* you have added bright colour to my world,
  - Little unborn baby *ABC*—you've already brought us great joy.
- My precious sisters in Christ, **Marto, Angie, Diordre, Aruni, Shira, Nelun, Nimali, Kumi, Sherreen, Leafy, Vasu, Rathy, Sandy, Helen, Anne Moldrich, Teruni, Dharshi Mendis, Karen Harrison, Sue, Joan, Anna, Jade, Mich** and **Jan.** Many of you live in far flung places but you will always remain close to my heart. Thank you so much for your love, friendship and prayers which have blessed me time and time again.
- **Pen(elope), Nola, Jenny Glazebrook, Jenny O'Hagan, Elaine, Paula, Adele, Melinda, Lesley, Jo'Anne & Rhonda,** my heart-warming writing buddies, you have helped fan the flames of

- my dreams and made them burn bright. You have taught me, encouraged me and prayed for me. My writing journey has been a lot of fun with you on board.
- Pastors **Jeff** and **Andy,** thank you so much for helping me experience God in deeper and glorious ways. Your godly examples have inspired me and blessed me.
- **Kumi, Anita, Aruni, Mama, Lorraine, Valerie, Gloria, Mich, Jan & Sylvia,** you've shared your unique stories in my book—I'm grateful to you for colouring the tapestry of my journey with Jesus with your own vibrant shades.
- **Prithiva, Melanie, Pamita, Dhaki, Ishani, Maheshini,** special friends of my childhood, you've blessed my journey. I thank God for you.
- **Armour Books** and **Anne Hamilton**—a special thank you to you for believing in my writing. It's been a joy to work with you and I'm deeply grateful.
- Finally and most importantly, my thanks are long and loud to my Saviour and Lord, the Lover of my soul, **Jesus.** You are my Strong Tower, my Strength and my Song. You are my Treasure. You loved me. You lavished your grace upon me. Because of Your Presence in my life I've learnt to keep *Dancing in the Rain.*

Contents

Prologue – *Letter to Golden Girl*	1
Poem 1 – *Dry my tears, Lord*	3
Oh No! It's Raining – Part 1	5
Oh No! It's Raining – Part 2	8
Little Nugget 1 – *Serenity Prayer*	12
Every Monday – *Part 1*	13
Friends' Stories 1 – *Kumi's Story*	15
My Story 1 – *Seasons*	17
Little Nuggets 2 – *God is…*	19
Poem 2 – *Mend Me, Lord*	21
I need an Umbrella – Part 1	23
Every Monday – *Part 2*	27
I need an Umbrella – Part 2	29
Friends' Stories 2 – *Anita's Story*	31
My Story 2 – *When God was silent*	33
Little Nuggets 3 – *Seven Nuggets of Wisdom to bless you*	36
Poem 3 – *I will trust You*	38
It's OK to grieve – Part 1	41
It's OK to grieve – Part 2	43
Every Monday – *Part 3*	47
Friends' Stories 3 – *Aruni's Story*	49
My Story 3 – *If it matters to you*	51

Little Nuggets 4 – *Thank you list*	53
Poem 4 – *His Love*	55
A Rainbow called HOPE – Part 1	**58**
A Rainbow called HOPE – Part 2	**61**
Every Monday – *Part 4*	65
Friends' Stories 4 – *Anne's Story*	67
My Story 4 – *There was a time*	69
Little Nuggets 5 – *Quotes that bless*	71
Poem 5 – *The Centre of Your Will*	73
Splashing through the puddles – Part 1	**75**
Splashing through the puddles – Part 2	**78**
Every Monday – *Part 5*	82
Friends' Stories 5 – *Lorraine's Story*	84
My Story 5 – *Winter of Rich Content*	87
Little Nuggets 6 – *Psalm 34*	88
Poem 6 – *There are Times*	92
Laughter, the Best Medicine – Part 1	**95**
Laughter, the Best Medicine – Part 2	**98**
Every Monday – *Part 6*	101
Friends' Stories 6 – *Valerie's Story*	103
My Story 6 – *The Bag*	105
Little Nuggets 7 – *Attitude – my Friend in times of grief*	107
Poem 7 – *Your Way, O Lord*	109
Tall Stories about Rainy Days – Part 1	**111**
Tall Stories about Rainy Days – Part 2	**115**
Every Monday – *Part 7*	118
Friends' Stories 7 – *Gloria's Story*	120

My Story 7 – *God Spaces*	122
Little Nuggets 8 – *Words that bring Hope and Healing*	123
Poem 8 – *Hope*	125
Sailing Paper Boats – Part 1	**129**
Sailing Paper Boats – Part 2	**133**
Every Monday – *Part 8*	137
Friends' Stories 8 – *Michelle's Story*	139
My Story 8 – *In front of the Mirror*	141
Little Nuggets 9 – *Praise List*	143
Poem 9 – *Season of Growth*	145
How Green is my Valley – Part 1	**148**
How Green is my Valley – Part 2	**151**
Every Monday – *Part 9*	155
Friend's Story 9 – *Sylvia's Story*	157
My Story 9 – *Unseen*	160
Little Nuggets 10 – *Wisdom for tough times*	161
Friends' Stories 10 – *Jan's Story*	164
Poem 10 – *The Darkest hour is before the Dawn*	166
And Best of All – Part 1	**170**
Every Monday – *Part 10*	174
And Best of All – Part 2	**175**

Dedication

*To my beloved husband Shan.
My partner in life's journey.*

*Thank you for making the stormy days brighter.
Thank you for dancing in the rain with me.*

I love doing life with you.

Prologue:

Dearest *Golden Girl*,

This book is for you. I pray it blesses you as much as it blessed me to write it. You once asked me what the point of life is when there is so much suffering. Whether there is any hope amidst the despair.

I told you then, 'Yes, there is hope. Yes, life does make sense even in the midst of suffering, GG.' I say it to you again today. Yes, life is complex. Stuff happens. Bad things happen to good people. But there *is* a huge point to our existence, even in the midst of our heartache and tears.

I am writing this book is to explain, if I can, the sense that I have made of life and sadness and suffering and God and the meaning of it all. As we go through life's journey, most of us face times of darkness, sadness and despair. Some face it much more than others. Sometimes, life hurts. It hurts a lot. Hurts too much. Often there are good people who are thrown into tough times. Life is inexplicable. Life is often unfair.

As a child of God, what do I do with those tough times? What does God require of me? Why does He permit them in the first place? Does He even care? Is there any hope at all?

Please take a journey with me, as we splash through the rain together. Often, during stormy seasons, all I might see is the grey dreary sky, the relentless rain, the menacing clouds forming overhead and a broken umbrella.

But GG dearest … I say again, there is hope.

Wishing you many beautiful rainbows after the rain—the kind that shines forever.

Loving you always,

Aunty Anu xo

Dry my tears, Lord

Poem 1

Lord,
I come to you,
Sad
Alone
Scared
Devastated.

What can I say, Lord?
You know me.
You know the inside of my heart.

You know my standing up and
my lying down.
You created me,
You formed me as I grew up.

Lord,
Have mercy on
me
Your child

I stay close
to You
wrapped in
the tender
blanket of
Your grace.

Finding
peace
and
comfort
In my troubled
times.

Seeking refuge
under
the shelter
of
Your wings.

Oh no! It's raining! – Part 1

Rainy Day Thoughts

Nightmare.

My husband and I and our son were living in Malaysia. We were enjoying my husband's sabbatical together in a foreign land. *Then...*

Our eight-year-old discovered an unusual growth in his mouth—a little soft white tissue between his cheek and back tooth. I took him to the dentist to check it out. Nervousness fluttered within me like a desperate butterfly trying to escape.

When the dentist looked uneasy, it shook me further. Alarm bells began to ring in my mind. Loud. Persistent. Urgent. I called my husband and we took Asela to see a specialist as soon as we could. Shan and I sat in his waiting room.

Thud, thud, thud. It was my heart but it sounded like a basketball bouncing on a tin roof.

The oral surgeon looked grave when he called us in. He told us the growth in Asela's mouth could be malignant. *Malignant? Was it cancer? Would we lose our precious little boy?*

Our world was crashing around us. We held hands and clung onto each other. In the surgeon's voice I could hear concern and fear. That immediately transferred dread into mine. *It could not be.*

Nightmare.

Several very traumatic weeks and one operation passed. Whom did I cling onto then? God. Yes, there was no one else who could hold me together. I didn't have much hope but I did have Him.

As our little boy was wheeled into the operation theatre for his operation, I was at the doorway. My husband wasn't permitted wait with me. I had my Bible. I turned to Psalm 91. I read it over and over again.

'He who dwells in the shelter of the Most High will abide in the shadow of the Almighty. I will say to the Lord, "My refuge and my fortress, my God, in whom I trust."' Psalm 91:1–2 NASB

God's Word was the Umbrella I needed. And so, I clung to it. I read some more: *'For you have made the Lord, my refuge, even the Most High, your dwelling place. No evil will befall you, nor will any plague come near your tent. For He will give His angels charge concerning you, to guard you in all your ways.'* Psalm 91:9–11 NASB

Yes, God had been our refuge. He was our dwelling place. He was holding out a precious promise to me during those difficult moments. His angels would be guarding my son. I had a hope to cling to.

'Because he has loved Me, therefore I will deliver him; I will set him securely on high, because he has known My name. He will call upon Me, and I will answer him; I will be with him in trouble; I will rescue him and honour him. With a long life I will satisfy him and let him see My salvation.' Psalm 91:14–16 NASB

I decided to rely fully on God. He would come through for me.

As suddenly and swiftly as the nightmare began, so it ended. The growth was found to be benign. *Thank you, God. Thank you God with all our hearts.*

Asela emerged triumphant. He was fine. Whole again. Our world began to straighten out. God had restored our little boy. Yes, we would have to monitor his health, but we had made it.

I know you, as you read this book, will have many such dates imprinted in your mind. Unlike the story I shared, you may have experienced a tragedy. Perhaps your nightmare has never ended. The death of a person you loved? An illness that left you gasping? An unfair job loss which stretched into a soul-destroying search for employment? Perhaps it was a betrayal by your best friend? A natural disaster that took away your home? A painful divorce not of your making? The breakdown of a relationship that changed your life forever?

Perhaps it is a series of little things that have gone on and on and on. And life has been sagging badly since, never picking up again.

Who among us has not suffered? Christian believers know life can be full of pain and that God sometimes calls us to suffer. Yes, strange as it may sound, suffering is meant to be part of our journey. The apostle Paul reminds us of this in the book of Philippians.

'For to you it has been granted for Christ's sake, not only to believe in Him, but also to suffer for His sake.' Philippians 1:29 NASB

My credentials for writing this book are few: first, I have lived life and known pain and suffering. But that is not all. *I have also known Jesus.* I have experienced His deep love which has held me together during tough seasons. I have known His peace reigning through nights when tears flowed. I have found His joy in the midst of pain. I have been blessed with healing as I've clung to Him.

And so, as we explore this topic—this perplexing, ambiguous and difficult subject of suffering, I ask our God to lead us. May His hope gleam brightly like a lighthouse that shines its radiance on dark and choppy seas to enable the ship of *Hope* to be safely brought to harbour.

Oh no! It's raining – Part 2

Rainy Day Thoughts

'Praise be to the God and Father of our Lord Jesus Christ. He is the Father who is full of mercy, the God of all comfort. He comforts us every time we have trouble so that when others have trouble, we can comfort them with the same comfort God gives us.' 2 Corinthians 1:3–4 ERV

Yes, the rain often falls though we'd rather have sunshine and blue skies. But as we seek God's word to us, I pray we will be blessed in the exploration. That He would enlighten us. Comfort us. Unite those who suffer. That you and I would always cling into Him, even when all seems lost. *Especially* when all seems lost. I pray that, as we go forth to a hurting world with what we learn and discover, God would use us to bring healing and to be a blessing to others.

The purpose of this book is not to wallow in suffering, hurt or grief. Wallowing in a mud puddle won't make us clean and shiny. Walking bravely with our umbrellas up is perhaps a better way of facing the rainy periods in life. Not that grieving isn't excluded. But we who know Jesus grieve differently to those who don't. We know the end of the story, after all! Romans 8:28 KJV assures us that all things work together for the good of those who are called by Him. And so, even as you and I suffer, we suffer in the context of having an umbrella over us. And the name of that umbrella? *Hope*.

As William L Watkinson reminds us, *Hope* is lighting a candle rather than cursing the darkness.

Hope is living with Eternity's perspective. Our hope is strong and sure:

- like the foundation of the house the wise man built, which held firm even while the storms raged
- like the beautiful butterfly emerging from a broken chrysalis
- like the spring that follows winter each year
- like the empty cross that led to resurrection joy

Suffering happens for different reasons. We suffer due to the sins of others. We suffer as a consequence of our own sin. We suffer as a mixture of both. We suffer because of a tainted world. Here are some questions that might arise in our minds when bad things happen.

- Why did she die so young?
- Why did You do this to me, Lord?
- What did I do to deserve this?
- Is there a purpose in this suffering, Lord?
- *Lord, do you even care?*

I have learned that God encourages my honest questions. He is a loving Father and His shoulders are big enough to accept my anger, my questions, my doubts and my discouragement. But then ... I have also discovered that the 'why' questions don't really take me anywhere. Other people have different experiences with 'why'. But I've learned to focus on God's promise to me that He will work things out for my best. He assures me He will be with me always. But He rarely explains Himself. That's what trust is all about, after all.

I dare answer the last of my questions today, not because of who I am but because of the One I know. The question was: *'Do you even care, Lord?'*

The answer is a resounding 'Yes'. God does care. He cares more than I realise. More than I can ever imagine. How do I know? The Bible tells us there is One Name above all others—the Name of Jesus. He has the answers to the many questions I ask of Him and the answers to the questions I don't.

He has all the answers. Full stop. He created the Universe. The world is held together by His Hands. He was before all things. He is the Alpha and Omega, the Beginning and the End. He came down to earth over 2000 years ago for the sole purpose of reconciling a lost world to fellowship with Him. Love was the motive behind His creation. Love was the purpose behind redemption. Love is the reason why God does what He does. Love is the reason you and I are alive today. And so, if I reply to that question, 'Does God even care?', my answer is … *yes*. A simple but powerful 'YES'.

Like most of us, I have experienced seasons when the winter rains were relentless, soaking me, making me gasp and shiver. There was a time when God seemed to take from my hands all that I prized dearly. First, I was forced to resign from a job I loved. Next, I had no choice but to leave a longstanding ministry which I was passionate about. Finally, I had to say goodbye to my dearly loved church family of 15 years. It was a very sad time.

As if that wasn't enough, two close friends passed away a few weeks later, one of them overnight in her sleep at the age of 43. Eight months afterwards, our home was in extreme danger of being burnt down by fires sweeping through our neighbouring suburbs. It was a terrifying few days. While in the midst of that crisis, my special unique lifetime friend, my one and only beloved mum—passed away in far off Sri Lanka, unexpectedly, after a brief illness. How sad I was that I didn't get a chance to bid her goodbye. I plunged into a season of grief and wept daily for months, missing her.

Many of the learning curves I share in this book are from situations like these, which turned my world upside down. For the past twelve years, I have struggled with a chronic illness. No matter how hard I have tried to get over it, the condition has only seemed to become more debilitating over the years. It has limited my life in numerous ways. It caused me to question God and to seek Him afresh. But the wonderful truth is that my times of suffering have not been in vain, They have brought me closer to Him—a precious gift that I would not exchange for all the riches of this world.

God has often showered me with His special brand of agápē love when I've been badly in need of it; when I didn't deserve it; when I was hurting; when the world seemed to turn its back on me; when I was sad and lonely and discouraged. This amazing agápē love, the 'love in spite of everything' gives me reason to hope. The hard times don't mean that God's love has turned away from me. It means I will discover more of His love as I cling to Him.

Agápē love is free, unconditional—undeserved—but always sure. It is a love we can count on. Not because of our goodness, but because God's infinite character is to love. He loves you. He loves me. All the time. Whenever life hurts. Especially when life hurts.

Will you dare believe it?

Yes, it's raining but we have a hope to cling to.

His name is Jesus. And He is love.

Little Nuggets 1

Nuggets to help me through those stormy seasons

The Serenity Prayer

*God grant me the serenity
to **accept** the things I cannot change;
courage to change the things I can;
and **wisdom** to know the difference.*

*Living one day at a time;
Enjoying one moment at a time;
Accepting hardships as the pathway to peace;
Taking, as He did, this sinful world
as it is, not as I would have it;*

*Trusting that He will make all things right
if I surrender to His Will;*

*That I may be reasonably happy in this life
and supremely happy with Him
Forever in the next.
Amen.*

Reinhold Niebuhr

Every Monday – Part 1

A little story in ten parts

The bell sounded loud and shrill in my ears and I woke up with a start. I glanced at the large oval clock on the wall. 10 minutes past 11. I must have dozed off. It was my day off; so I'd taken it easy. I hadn't slept too well, the same as it had been for many nights now. No wonder I had drifted off. Slowly, unwillingly … I got up.

The bell shrieked again. Then silence. I walked with halting steps to the front door, a sudden mad hope in my heart. What if I found Peter on the other side of the door? What if he stood there with his dazzling smile, his shock of black hair blowing in the wind, his dark eyes glowing?

As if. As if it could happen. Peter, my dearly loved husband of 33 years, 7 months and 2 days was not going to be there. It was two whole weeks since he had died. Peter, my high school sweet heart, my lover, my best friend. Peter, the one person on earth who understood me; who accepted me and knew me inside out. He was dead. Peter of the warm heart and open mind. Peter of the broad shoulders and a smile in his voice. Peter, the proud father of my three children. He would never be coming home again. Never.

The key didn't turn at once. Perhaps it was because my fingers felt like jelly. I finally managed to turn it. I opened the front door. I didn't know whom to expect. Nor did I care. I looked out of my screen door. There was no one to be seen.

But on the ground, on the large green welcome mat, lay one long stemmed red rose. It was as red as the blood that had been pumped into my husband's veins a week before he died.

I rubbed my eyes. *Was it really there?* I bent down and picked it up. A dark crimson centre with soft deep red petals. A scent that was delicate and fragrant. Who could have put it there? I noticed a little slip of paper on the ground and I picked it up.

There were two words typed in clear black font. *"Next Monday!"*

...to be continued

Kumi's Story

Friends' Stories – 1

It was one of those mornings when everything seemed to go so wrong. Grouchy, whining children late for school; half a dozen things still to be done before they left. The girls needed to get to school earlier than usual because they were acting in a play. One had to go, already dressed in her costume. She was supposed to change into her school uniform after the performance.

My husband had been very impatient with them. 'If you get any later, I'll leave you and go off to work. Hurry up.'

Unfortunately, it had very little effect. But finally, they were ready. Armed with hand-made props too large for them to carry and with three extra bags, they trooped outside. They piled into our vehicle and it sped off. I went back inside.

To my dismay, I found my younger daughter's white socks. They were the pair she was to change into after the play. I hit the panic button. I didn't dare call my already irate husband. He *certainly* would *not* have returned to collect the socks. Worried, I called eight mums who lived close by the school to ask if they could take an extra pair of socks for my little girl. But, as luck would have it, I couldn't reach a single one of them.

Regrets played through my mind like the reel of a bad movie. Waves of helplessness washed over me. I'd been very weary for a while. That day, this small oversight seemed to magnify the word FAILURE. I stood at my front door with my baby's pair of socks in my hand, my mind a total blank. My heart was as heavy as a bag filled with rocks.

I heard the sound of a vehicle drive up to my gate. I heard the doorbell ring. I mechanically went to the gate and opened it. There on the other side of our tall black gate stood my dearest friend from childhood. She was on her way to work. She had suddenly remembered she needed to pick up a book from me and decided to come over at once.

I wasted no time with niceties. 'Please go to school and hand this over.'

She asked no questions. She turned around and went as quickly as she could. She told me later what had occurred. Her pre-arranged office transport had come for her early that morning as usual. She had felt too lazy to go with it and instead she'd phoned later for a taxi. She was passing my lane and had felt a strong urge to come to my home. The book could have waited as it wasn't urgent.

'God works in mysterious ways, doesn't He?' She smiled at me.

God let me know He loved me, that He is watching out for my little girl … through a simple pair of socks. Even if a mother forgets her child, God will not forget—just as we read in the Word. If we just realise it more often we would know without a shadow of doubt that nothing in our lives, nothing at all … is too insignificant for God to notice.

Seasons

My Stories – 1

I stood outdoors waving at my husband. It has always been our little morning ritual as he leaves for work—two waves accompanied by smiles. The first wave as Shan reaches the road; the next at the end of our street, just before he disappears off my horizon.

After he left, I stood a little longer, surveying the chilly landscape. It was technically the last day of autumn. However it was obvious winter had already arrived as I gazed at the tree in our front yard, bereft of all its leaves. Rather sad, to see it stark and naked against the drab sky. I'd delighted in it all autumn as its lush green garb changed into picturesque yellow attire. I'd watched its butter-coloured leaves flutter to the ground—creating a pretty golden carpet.

But today, I felt dejected as I looked at it. Its form was stark. Cold. Naked. Death looked at me through the cheerless, undressed branches. And then I thought back to my recent past. I had experienced change. A few of my close friendships had changed. It had been very sudden. Unexpected. I hadn't seen it coming. But then change in most spheres of life is inevitable, isn't it?

As I gazed at the tree, I knew that, in three brief months, new shoots would appear. Soft pastel green buds would grow a little more every day. They would cover the tree. As I thought about it, I knew my life would follow a similar pattern. Yes, those friendships may have died right now. But perhaps what had really occurred was transformation.

I knew what I had to do. I had to let go. To embrace change. To make good come out of unpleasant events. Out of the death of these friendships would come something wholesome, something better. Perhaps other friendships would replace them. Perhaps these friendships might rekindle—in a new and better way.

As sure as the passing of seasons, I knew that all God permitted in my life was for good. People may let me down. Friends might hurt me. But nothing ever happened without my loving Father's knowledge. I could rest in that because His ways always worked for good in my life. *Always.*

And so that morning, while nursing my bruised, sad, rejected heart, I also carried hope within me. A heart that embraced change, because—while my heart grieved—my head assured me that change is good. Even necessary. He allows difficult things to occur in order for Him to do His perfect work in me.

No Death? No Life!
No change? No Miracle!
No Calvary? No Resurrection!

Little Nuggets 2

Nuggets to help me through those stormy seasons

God is…

- God is my Best Musician—He makes my heart sing.

- God is the Book I will never stop reading—blessing me with contentment, smiles, laughter, joy.

- God is the Smile in my heart that grows wider and wider every passing day.

- God is my Covering—I feel snug and warm in Him.

- God is the Living Water of the stream that ripples and flows and adds so much life to my day.

- God is the Song in my Guitar as it plays a million chords of new music and still has incalculable new songs to be played.

- God is the Painter of sunsets glowing in the sky—filling my heart with wonder and joy.

- God is the Light in my glasses helping me see the world in ways I had not imagined before.

- God is the amazing Manuscript I read, filled with fresh wisdom and insight.

- God is the Morning and Evening Star, shining brighter each night as I gaze on the heavens.

- God is the Huge Boulder I hide behind when the enemy jumps into my path.

- God is my perfect Dancing Partner—He puts a spring in my step, He holds me, He leads me.

- God is the Eagle flying high who swoops down and carries me to safety when I need Him.

- God is the Rainbow in my sky after the rains and the storms, bringing colour and bright *hope* to my world!

Mend Me, Lord

A million pieces
Broken
Shattered
Strewn
All over …
Everywhere.

That's what I am now, Lord
Spent,
Sad,
Hurting.

A porcelain vase
Broken
Beyond repair
Its parts lying
Everywhere.
Too many,
Too many.
Too many to count or pick up.
Too many to put together.

Heal me, Lord.
I need Your touch,
Your Love
Your Comfort
Your Peace.

I wait
In stillness,
And
In hope,
Knowing
That in spite of life
Its hurt
And its pain,
In spite of hard moments
And broken dreams,
It will be all right.

Knowing full well
That when I touch
The hem of your garment,
I shall be whole again.

I need an umbrella! – Part 1

Umbrellas of hope to protect me through rainy days

My life was cruising along at the speed limit, safe, secure and sure ... when, without warning, the speedometer cracked and everything came to a standstill. The rain started. It pelted down thick and fast. I was in pain. In deep sadness. In despair. And the torrent wouldn't stop. It rained relentlessly on and on and on.

I needed an umbrella.

Three months later, I was able to look back with gladness. Three months later, I was glad to have been in God's training school, but that day—I wasn't. I was shocked. Bruised. Broken. Hurting. Not knowing if I could get up again. I am sure all of us have been in that place. The times when life suddenly throws us a dozen lemons. And expects us to make lemonade?

What do you when sour stuff happens—when life is unbearable? Can you get off the world till the storm subsides? It would be good if we could, don't you think? This is how I coped—I told myself over and over again that I'd be okay. I clung onto hope, even though it was such a thin and fragile thread it would have broken in the tiniest waft of breeze. On the outside I functioned quite well. But on the inside, a deep sinking feeling had taken up residence. It would not go away, no matter how much I reasoned with it.

What did I do? I cried a lot. I turned to God. I listened to Him—*really* listened.

I turned to His Word. I read the Book as if my life depended on it. As indeed it did. I talked daily to my husband whose loving empathy blessed me.

Healing didn't come fast enough for me. But it did come. The pain didn't go away all at once, but I was on my way to healing, one day at a time.

When the rainy seasons arrive, you and I find ways we get through them, don't we? I wonder what you use to get through those grey seasons. Perhaps you try to sleep away the pain. Perhaps you yell at God and tell Him what you think of Him. You ask Him where He is; you question Him, wanting to know if He even cares. Perhaps you kick a chair till it breaks or smash a few glasses? Or shout at those closest to you? Perhaps you keep the pain to yourself and continue living nobly? Do you act as if nothing is wrong, when in fact you feel you've woken up to a nightmare?

Sometimes, we turn to things that may help us in the short term but in the long term would hurt us even more. Numbing the pain may work for a while, but reality will eventually hit without warning. Chasing after transient pleasures might help temporarily but afterwards comes the reckoning.

Breaking a few glasses might help in the short term but clearing up broken glass is no fun.

Once, to vent my frustration, I threw a glass down and broke it. I learnt a good lesson. *Never break a glass—no matter how angry I feel.* I spent hours looking for the broken splinters. The time and effort to clear the mess wasn't worth the emotional release I gained. No—I have never broken a glass since!

When I faced a season in my life after my world caved in, I was resolute in my prayers that I would not sin. I had come to this difficult place, chiefly due to what others had done. But when I reflected on events, I realised that I too had been wrong in my responses. I was therefore determined to take steps to walk in integrity. To walk as close to God as I could. To turn to Him alone for healing.

And so I looked for some solid umbrellas I could use, to prevent the rain from soaking me. I found them, and they helped keep the rain off my hair. They helped me keep walking while the rain poured down. And brought me the tonic I needed.

Here are some of the 'brollies' that I used and found helpful to take me from a place of despair into a place of rest and hope.

1. The love of family and friends
2. Christian music
3. Chocolates (in moderation)
4. Time with God / prayer
5. Tears
6. Being alone
7. Walking
8. Composing poems
9. Composing songs
10. Keeping busy
11. Helping people
12. Soaking in the Word

Sometimes these things helped. Sometimes, they didn't. Sometimes *nothing* helped. But I pieced my life together one day at a time. They each added something significant into my life. I'm sure you could add your own ideas to mine. Perhaps you like doing craft and find healing while you create something beautiful? Or you clean out your house to keep yourself busy? Do you paint— painting is great therapy. Perhaps you like to ride your bike? Or go sailing?

Perhaps you fix things around your home? Or go scuba diving? Perhaps you like to disappear somewhere on your own to hike, to think, to pray? Do you go fossicking? Or do you indulge in some brisk bungee-jumping?

Whatever means you use, it may be a good idea to have your ideas ready. That way, when the rainy times happen, you have a helpful list to whisk out for your use.

Did the rains arrive, my friend?

Every Monday – Part 2

A little story in ten parts

I frowned and shook my head in disbelief. I walked back inside. Like a slow moving robot, I opened my kitchen cupboard. In measured deliberate movements, I took out the beautiful cut-glass vase my sister Veronica had given me last Christmas.

I filled it with water. I placed my single rose into it. I looked at it with my eyes focussed far away. It was then the dam burst and the tears came. My blouse was soaked but I didn't care. There was despair, there was sadness, there was grief, there was anger. There was loneliness; there was regret. There was guilt. Why did Peter die? Why not me instead? I wept.

Why did Peter have to die? He was only 53. He had more living left to do. Lots more living. The cancer had struck without warning. Three months after his diagnosis, he was dead of a malignant brain tumour. My Peter of the mischievous smile and a hundred questions would not be home again. My Peter of the impish ways and loving heart was no more. My Peter who annoyed me by the way he left drawers pulled out, his socks thrown all over our room or by talking to me when I longed for silence … my Peter was no more. Oh, if he would come back, I would never complain about anything he did again. Never! But it was too late now.

Over the next few days, I gazed at the rose many times. I didn't try to reason who'd put it there. Perhaps it was a neighbour trying to be kind. Perhaps one of my children had brought it over. But none of them admitted to placing the rose on my front porch. I was too tired to care. Peter had brought me a single red rose every Mother's day. And so … this dark red rose soothed my heart in a strange, painful, bittersweet way.

The next Monday, I was talking on the phone, when the doorbell rang again. This time it was at 2 minutes past 2. I looked up. Startled. *Another red rose?* 'There's someone at the front door,' I said and hung up. I was glad of the intrusion. I didn't really want to talk to Aunt Martha who dissected Peter's death so much it made me want to scream. I reached the front door and opened it. The sun was filtering through the large gum trees in the front yard. The grass was overgrown. It was time to mow the lawn again. Peter would never mow our lawn again, would he?

No one stood there. But on the doormat lay something. Once more. Not a long stemmed red rose this time. But a little square package wrapped up in bright green cellophane. It was tied in a soft, silky, deep green ribbon. Next to the package was a little slip of paper with two words printed on it: '*Next Monday*'.

I took the package inside and opened it. With trembling fingers I undid the ribbon. I tore open the cellophane. Wide-eyed, I took out the little music box that nestled inside. As I opened the lid and a tune started to play. A little cute smiling girl with raven black hair and an orange can-can skirt, twirled around as the music played. 'You are my sunshine… my only sunshine.' The enchanting tinkling melody rang sweetly on and on.

…to be continued

I need an umbrella! – Part 2

Umbrellas of hope that will protect me through those rainy days

I have an umbrella I'd recommend at *all* times. We need hope when the rain gushes down. Hope that the rains will eventually stop. Hope that the floods won't overwhelm us. Hope that the rain will bring us a rainbow. Hope that one day the sun will shine again.

God's word tells us we have a hope that is indestructible.

'Guide me in Your truth and teach me, for you are God my Saviour, and my hope is in You all day long.' Psalm 25:5 NIV

'Be strong and let your heart take courage, all you who hope in the Lord.' Psalm 31:24 NASB

'But the eyes of the Lord are on those who fear Him, on those whose hope is in His unfailing love.' Psalm 33:18 NIV

'How blessed is he whose help is the God of Jacob, whose hope is in the Lord his God.' Psalm 146:5 NASB

'Eat honey, dear child—it's good for you— and delicacies that melt in your mouth. Likewise knowledge, and wisdom for your soul—get that and your future's secured, your hope is on solid rock.' Proverbs 24:14 (The Message)

Once, when I faced a crisis in my life, I turned to a close friend—but sadly she couldn't understand. She couldn't help me. That hurt so much. But through that experience God taught me a hard lesson and a sweet one. *'Come to Me,'* He said to my sad heart, over and over again. *'I am all you need.'* The problem is that I usually prefer to run to someone with skin on. I yearn for flesh and blood to hold me in their heart.

But God's lessons through that stormy period were sure. And lessons I needed to learn.

And so God became my Special Umbrella—my Shelter from the storm. Later, He sent me a few beautiful caring friends to walk the rest of my journey. But first, I had to learn the importance of leaning only on Him. How grateful I am now for this lesson, despite the fact that, at the time, I baulked at it.

Yes, God has been my Rock and Hiding place over the stormy seasons. My Strong Tower. My Strength and my Refuge. He was my special Umbrella. My Shelter from the storm.

May I lend you my Brolly?

Anita's Story

Friends' Stories 2

It happened during my wedding preparations. Close to D-day, we ran short of money. So I decided to do away with the reception. However my fiancé Steve felt we should host a wedding lunch—but only for the immediate family. I didn't have the money to spend even on that, so I was very unhappy. That week in the office, a staffer talked to me about his pastor. He said he was very poorly paid.

The next Sunday while walking to church I was thinking about our finances. I brushed away a few tears. The preacher that morning was the pastor my colleague had mentioned. He spoke from Matthew 6:25–34. *'Do not be anxious…'* His sermon spoke directly to me and my burden lifted. God gave me the power and strength to let go of the anxiety about our wedding plans.

On Monday when I reached home after work, my Mum told me that a stranger had come to our home and given her an envelope with cash inside. Such a thing had never occurred to us before. We weren't sure whether this was meant for us or for someone else, so we didn't use the money but kept it aside.

A few days later, a letter came from Canada from one of our former neighbours. They had lived near us for four years. In it they had mentioned that the money was for us. The following lines from that letter meant even more to me than the gift itself. This is what it said. *'The God you worship wanted us to send this gift to you.'*

Even today, many years on, tears of joy fill my eyes whenever I recall the incident.

God is a gracious Father and a wonderful Provider. I thank Him with all my heart.

When God was Silent

My Stories – 2

It had been a difficult day. Everything had gone wrong. I had been hurt. I felt sad and alone. And so ... I went to God. For comfort. For succour. For strength. Heart-sick, weary and sad, I clung to Him. *'God, are you there? God, do you care? God, do you hear me?'*

Usually when I'm hurting, I hear His whispers in my heart; I feel His soft caress. But this time was different. There was total silence. I turned to my daily dose of Facebook. As I scrolled through it, I thought I heard God speak. *'For I know the plans I have for you,' declares the Lord, 'plans to prosper you and not to harm you, plans to give you hope and a future.'* (Jeremiah 29:11 NIV)

My spiritual ears pricked up. I read on. As I looked further, there came the identical promise again but the words were slightly different. *'For I know the thoughts that I think toward you,' says the Lord, 'thoughts of peace and not of evil, to give you a future and a hope.'* (Jeremiah 29:11 NKJV)

A little breeze of comfort fanned me. Was that God speaking to me? The promises above were ones I'd been claiming earlier for the very situation I was sad about. And so I wrote in my journal.

'You said it twice to me today. Thank You, Lord. Please let someone else send me this verse too. Please? So it is re-assurance to me that it's YOUR word to me.' I knew God would honour my prayer. *Or would He?* And did I get what I'd

asked God for? No. Not in the way I wanted. I knew He could have done it. But He chose not to. Or perhaps He did nudge someone, but they were too preoccupied to hear it? I don't know. I do know that I felt cheated and betrayed. By God Himself. Surely He could do this little thing for me? I wasn't asking Him to do anything big. I didn't ask Him to change my situation. I didn't ask Him to explain why things were the way they were. All I asked for was a bit of encouragement from someone. *Anyone.*

But the only response I received was total silence.

On my way back from my grocery shopping that day, heartsick and weary, I gave in to God. *'Lord—please speak to me. Not in the way I expect. But in the way YOU choose.'*

Immediately He flashed a breathtaking sunset into my vision—a love-message in pictures. Large white cotton clouds silhouetted against a dark, deepening evening sky. What made it unique was that each cloud had a lining. The proverbial cloud with a silver lining? No. This was even better. *The lining was golden.* In spite of my sadness, I had to smile. *'Thank you, Lord. You win. You did speak to me but in a method of Your choosing. Fair enough ... Fair enough.'*

And I believe that the Lord smiled back.

What did the Lord convey to me through this picture? That He who creates all things—that He, the author of such amazing beauty—that He, the Only Lord God—the Creator of heaven and earth, was in control and in charge of my future. And so He asked me to trust Him. Perhaps there was a smaller secondary message too. That every cloud God brings my way has a *Golden* lining? I've often seen those golden linings and yes, they've always shone. Brightly.

I'd hoped to receive a three-fold promise. But I didn't get Jeremiah 29:11–13 times three that day. However I did receive Three Messages from Him that conveyed the same promise—because over the next two days, He spoke to me through two more aspects of creation. I knew then. That He cared. That He is sovereign. And yes, that I could fully trust Him.

Little Nuggets 3

Nuggets to help me through those stormy seasons

Seven Nuggets of Wisdom to bless you

1. Smile—even if you feel sad. Look at the mirror often give yourself a bright grin. The endorphins released will help you feel better.

2. Write a list of the blessings you *do* enjoy. Read them every day. Thank God as you read them.

3. As you wake up each morning, find three reasons to thank God and to praise Him. At the end of each day, do the same. In between, sandwich the day with praise and thanks. Yes, sprinkle your day with spots of praise and larger pools of praise.

4. Think of what happened to you as something temporary. Think of what occurred as one part of your life; not your whole life. Don't blame yourself for what happened. If you need forgiveness, turn to our compassionate Father. His forgiveness is yours. If it's someone else's fault, be willing to forgive.

5. Ask God what He is teaching you through your circumstance. It will immediately turn into something positive and beneficial.

6. Remind yourself: *'This too shall pass.'* It will.

7. Put the word **REMEMBER** up somewhere. *Remember* good things.

I will trust you

Poem 3

Tears and sadness
Questions
Asking,
Waiting,
Sad
And troubled.
Perplexed at answers that
Don't add up.

Lord,
I don't
Understand
Any of it.

But I do know
That
You love me.
I do know
I can trust You,
I have known You
To be faithful

Not just once, but
Over and over and over again.

You do wonders
Far more than tongue can tell.
You create
A well of life
Out of a troubled heart.
Joy
Out of tears.
Beauty
Out of discord.
Jewels
Out of ugliness.
Your Perfect Peace
Through strife.

And so today,
I bring a heart of trust
To you my King.

I bring an offering
Of worship
To You my Lord;

I bring my heart
Splintered and broken
Many times over
But then put
Together anew by
Your unfathomable love.

I praise You Father God
For you have been
My all
And You remain.
Unchangeable.
Yesterday, Today
And forever

Jesus
The Faithful One
My Comforter
My Friend.
The Strong Tower
I can run to
And wait within,
Until the storm subsides.
I come to You,
I will trust you
And wait.

For You
O Lord
Make all things
Beautiful
In your time!

It's OK to grieve! – Part I

Tears are ok. Tears are good. Tears bring healing

I remember a time I wasn't allowed to grieve.

There was a time when life had had been filled with pain. And then, when the final storm arrived, crashing wildly into my life, I fell down with a very hard thud. And I couldn't get up for ages. I had to stop. For a breather. I had to grieve. Deeply. And for many months.

Have you ever been in a place like that? There are times I am strong and I can keep going no matter what occurs in my life. There are other times when I fold up in a fall that goes on and on, like one little domino in a set which when touched lightly, makes them all to fold over one by one. Like a kite that has lost its thread and comes hurtling down. Like a candle that is quickly snuffed out by a soft summer breeze. Like a sad child who has lost her favourite, much-loved pet.

People around us often mean well. But you know what? They often don't know anything about grieving. They might invite you places, trying to jolly you out of your grief. They may try to downplay your feelings, saying, 'It's time you started living again.' They might share exciting stories about their lives, hinting that, if you wanted to, you could do much better. Yes, they mean well. But they can hurt you even more.

Often, what you need when you're down and hurting is someone to accept and love you just the way you are. More important than any advice is a caring friend who is simply *'there for you'*—a friend who listens to you, understands the place you are at, allows you to talk about your grief, and allows you to walk the dark path you are on without condemnation or reproach.

Yes, people mean well. But it's easy enough not to understand another's suffering. It's easy when times are good to forget the bad times. It's easy when things are going well for us to look with judgment on those who are down. But if this book should say something at all—let it say this. It is ok to grieve. Grieving is not a sin. Grieving can bring healing. Grieving can actually be good for your soul.

With what authority do I say this? With the authority of one who has been there and done that. With the authority of one whose tears had meaning and helped her heal. With the authority of one who has at different times in her life spent hours at the feet of Jesus; soaking in His comfort, shedding tears but also receiving healing. In His school. And with His approval.

Yes, it is ok to grieve.

It's OK to grieve! – Part 2

Tears are OK. Tears are good. Tears bring healing.

Why is grieving important? Why is grieving necessary? How does it bring healing? I am no counsellor or psychologist. But… I have lived. I have known grief and pain. I've come out on the other side whole and happy again. And so I have seen what value there are in periods of grief when I don't deny my pain but acknowledge it. When I allow myself to hurt. When I think about the past in God's presence. When I shed tears that bring release.

Physical wounds take time to heal, don't they? It is the same, I believe, with our emotional and spiritual wounds. Just pretending they are not there will not make them disappear. Acknowledging their presence is the first step towards healing those wounds.

So yes, it's perfectly ok to grieve.

Who among us hasn't lost something or someone significant? Life on this planet involves loss—all the time. There's the loss of a loved one through death. I remember losing a puppy when I was 15 years old. My little doggy—Black Power or BP—had a very special place in my heart. I placed flowers on his grave every day when I came home after school. Sitting there grief stricken, I let my tears fall. His little bouncy vibrant puppy dog life had ended far too quickly.

We suffer loss through divorce—a wound that does not close in a hurry.

Miscarriage brings an extra tough kind of pain since the world has not seen your child and often doesn't understand your grief.

There's also rejection by loved ones. Or rejection from friends. Rejection from a group. Rejection from society.

The loss of a cherished dream can well cause sadness. Failure might bring us grief too hard to bear. Loss of financial stability is tough. Any change is often difficult and brings angst. I remember the homesickness I suffered when I first lived overseas. Learning to live in a new culture very different to my own was a huge challenge. I felt I had lost everything familiar—my extended family, my friends, my place in society, my job, my identity. The loneliness was relentless. It took a good 18 months before I started feeling 'normal' again.

The loss of your health can be devastating. Perhaps your life has changed drastically since you became sick and no one—not even those closest to you—can really empathise with you? Losing a job can be life-shattering. Your financial stability often comes with your job. Your self-respect can be tied to your job. Your respect from others could come from your job. So yes, losing your job can make you feel like a nobody.

Another big loss that may incur grief is of course relationship breakup. Good relationships give us a sense of self-worth and well-being. Relationship breakdown is the opposite of that, so your sense of purpose and hope in life can fly out of the window when a relationship ends.

There are many other ways loss comes to us. Giving birth to a child you think is perfect but has disabilities—hidden or otherwise—can be life-shattering. And then, old age brings its own share of loss and heartache. The world is too busy for older people. Loss of respect, loss of your faculties, loss of your independence. How hard it is. The list goes on. Sometimes grief may arrive through a series of difficulties in life that seem to stretch on and on for years on end.

Sadly, life is no picnic. *So yes my friend, it's ok to grieve.*

What are healthy ways of grieving then? How does grieving help? What would happen if we don't grieve? How long should we grieve? There are differing stages of grief and, although they may come in any order, it's helpful to think of stages.

The first stage of grief is *denial*. You find the situation hard to believe. 'This can't be happening,' you think. This is followed by deep *anger* and you want to blame someone. You feel frustrated and out of control. After anger comes d*epression*. You might think: 'If only this didn't happen' or 'If only I didn't do this' or 'I wish it would change' or 'I don't want to live any more.'

There's good news for us who grieve. Grief does not go on forever. The final stage of grief is *acceptance*. The time it takes from one stage to another will of course differ from individual to individual and from circumstance to circumstance. So do not despair if it's taking time to work through your grief.

It's ok to grieve!

There's a danger that grief that is not acknowledged could cause deeper wounds. Where trust existed, doubt and despair may take up residence. Where there was hope in life and hope in God, there now might be cynicism. Even a host of physical ailments could arrive if your grief is unresolved.

So yes, it's ok to grieve.

When I once turned to close friend during a season of grief, she didn't understand. She hurt me more by ignoring my pain, asking me to get over it and implying I had nothing to cry about. I'm sure she meant well and obviously had no inkling what I needed. One day, several weeks after I plunged into this season, I turned to a different friend. As I shared my story, my hurt and my pain into her listening ears, she was there for me. She held on to me. She loved me. I was allowed to grieve at last. How good that felt.

She accepted me, grief and all. That was what I had been yearning for. And what I needed. Thank God for friends who are God with skin on for us. It was the start of my healing.

Yes, it is ok to grieve.

Every Monday – Part 3

A little story in ten parts

I gazed at it, speechless, a lump in my throat. *'You are my sunshine.'* It was the song Peter sang to me when he teased me. Who put this music box on my front porch? No one else knew about our song. Not even the children. It had been a secret between us. Perhaps the children did know about it? Did *they* bring it over?

'No, Mum. It certainly wasn't me,' Michelle said when I asked her. 'It must be a mystery admirer.'

I tried to smile at that, but my mouth twisted downwards instead and my bottom lip quivered. I battled tears. My throat suddenly had a huge painful lump inside.

'Mum, are you ok?" Michelle's concerned voice came through the telephone. She was 26, very busy with her job at an advertising firm. A good kid. They all were good kids, all three of them. Their Dad was very proud of them. *When he was alive.*

'Thanks darling,' I whispered. It was very hard to get my voice working. 'I'm fine.' I called off quickly.

Would I ever be fine again? My beloved Pete was dead. My life had ended. No more waking up to a 'Hello Sleepyhead' in my husband's teasing voice. No more walks in the moonlight with him. No more dancing together after dinner to Strauss waltzes. No more sharing a chair and reading stories together. No more deep conversations. No more nothing. Peter was dead. And nothing would bring him back. But every Monday morning or afternoon or evening the doorbell rang. And on the welcome mat was always something different.

Once, there was a striking cashmere sweater in a deep mauve, my favourite colour. It fitted me perfectly. Another time, there was a book. Peter and I had read *Daddy Long Legs* by Jean Webster during our honeymoon. It was one of my favourites. My first copy—a gift from my parents—was coming apart so I was glad to get a new one.

One Monday there was a packet of Tim Tams—my favourite biscuit. I ate them all greedily; almost as if by finishing the packet, Peter would be brought back to life. *Strange*, I thought in retrospect. I had hardly eaten since the funeral. But my appetite picked up after that gift.

One Monday, there was a little Christmas bon-bon. I waited till my son's family visited, before I pulled it with Keith, my little grandson. Inside was a sewing kit. My grandson's excitement made me smile. 'Grandma needs to learn to sew, doesn't she, Keith?' I said. Little Keith chanted, 'Grandma sew. Grandma sew,' and danced around me.

I remembered Peter patiently taking his trousers in hand when they needed adjustment. He knew it would take a long long time for me to pick up a needle and thread. My Peter always understood. Or almost always. No, he wasn't perfect. But he was good enough for me. We had fitted each other perfectly. *We had been chums.*

… to be continued

Aruni's Story

Friends' Stories 3

We were holidaying in my home country, Sri Lanka, and had spent a few days with my husband's family in the southern city of Galle. We were about five minutes away from the Galle city centre, on our way to Colombo, when my sister-in-law suddenly suggested we all recite Psalm 91 together. I was a little surprised, but I didn't say anything. Instead we read and claimed the psalm together.

He who dwells in the shelter of the Most High
Will abide in the shadow of the Almighty.

I will say to the Lord, 'My refuge and my fortress,
My God, in whom I trust!'

…You will not be afraid of the terror by night,
Or of the arrow that flies by day;

… A thousand may fall at your side
And ten thousand at your right hand,
But it shall not approach you…

For you have made the Lord, my refuge,
Even the Most High, your dwelling place.

No sooner had we closed the Bible than with shocked eyes and pounding hearts we saw a massive wave of the sea speeding inland towards us. It was a tsunami. The waves were everywhere—they were behind us, they were in front of us. People were being tossed around. Boats suddenly appeared in our line of vision.

As our car sped on, a road to our right opened up leading inland. Dazed, my husband turned the car and went along that detour. Taking that path saved our lives. We barely made it, but we did escape the waves. I looked back in horror. The car behind us struggled through the water but thankfully managed to make it through. But my eyes opened wide when the one just behind it was simply swept away. Terror struck me. *Would we make it?*

A few hours later, we arrived in Colombo, alive, but numb with shock. We realised with great consternation that many others had not made it. They were dark days in our little island. I was very grateful to God that our lives were spared.

The words of Psalm 91 rang in my mind for days afterwards. God's promise is true. He is our shelter and our strong rock and refuge. His Word tells us that we will go through the water but it will not overwhelm us. The water didn't overwhelm us that day, even as we clung onto His promises. As the Psalmist proclaims, I too will say of the Lord, He is my refuge and my fortress, in Him will I trust.

If it matters to you

My Stories – 3

My friend and I came together to pray. We'd spent an hour chatting and catching up and now it was time to talk to God. A precious hour it was. We clicked easily because of our love for Jesus. Our weekly time together enriched our lives, as we shared the intricate ways that God cared for us.

That particular day though, as we finished praying and hugged each other goodbye, I felt a tinge of sadness. After I waved her off, I began to realise why I felt so unhappy. I hadn't felt understood. I'd agreed with what she'd said, but it wasn't what I really wanted to hear that day. I'd shared a concern. I'd told her that I felt sad. What would have helped me most was if she said, *'Yes, it's tough, isn't it?'* Or just an *'I'm sorry.'* I was hurting. And sometimes, just sometimes, I didn't want to discuss it in logical terms. I wanted a friend to say: *'I feel your pain.'*

I can't complain. My friend was being wise. And realistic. She'd said that what occurred would be good for me. Perhaps she was right. The problem though was that I didn't get the empathy I craved. As the day continued the sadness remained. I knew I was being silly. I knew she was right in what she said. But I just wanted to feel that someone understood. I went home and put my computer on when my eyes fell on a little card which I'd kept on my desk—just by my computer screen.

If it matters to you, it matters to Jesus.

The words jumped out of the card and blessed me—a fresh refreshing breeze which blew away the exhaustion of a difficult day. It brought balm to my sad heart. It was exactly what I'd been wanting to hear all day, that Someone Else knew my sadness and that He cared. I didn't need a lot of advice. I knew that all things worked together for the good for those who love God. My heart had been hungering so much to know that there was someone in the world who knew my feelings that day and validated them.

I found that Person. It wasn't any old friend. It was my Best Friend. If it matters to you, it matters to the One who created You; the One who came to give you life in all its fullness, the One whose love for you is boundless.

If it matters to you, it matters to Jesus.

Little Nuggets 4

Nuggets to help me through those stormy seasons

Here is a general list of THANKS that most of us can offer.
Make your own list out of it. Make it specific for yourself.
Remove ones that don't make sense to you and add new ones that do.

Thank you God for ...

Your love for me	Life	Health and strength
Eyes to see with	Ears to hear with	Feet to walk with
Hands to use	Food	Clothing
Computers	Modern Technology	My home
Good times	Laughter	Music and song
Simple joys	Books	Each new day
Sleep and rest	Holidays	Friends
Changing seasons	Hope	Beauty
Fun times	Pets	Nature
Things to do	Work	Play
Joyful times	Kind folk	Doctors
Blessings	Words	Poetry
Your Word	Your Promises	Your Faithfulness

His Love

Poem 4

There are times
of deep pain
in our lives.
Moments when time itself
stands still,
When we look back
with sadness,
Overwhelmed,
tearful
tested
trialled
taught by Him,
waiting.

There are times I've needed God
more than I did before.
Times when only God's
love was sure.
No other.
Constant
as the sun that rises each day.

At those moments
I run to my Father
And He runs towards me
Arms outstretched
To His daughter

He welcomes me back
With hugs
with grace
His warm embrace
His cloak
of beauty
which He places
on my shoulders.

I draw close
into His arms
Thankful
oh so thankful that
He never condemns,
only cares.

That His smile
is warm
and radiant,
lasting
in spite
of all
I am,
all I may have done
to hurt Him,

*the many times
I have disappointed Him.*

*I am thankful
for every second chance
He gives me
Thankful
that nothing I could do
would make Him love me more,
and nothing I could do
Would make Him love me less.*

*His love
is always enough
and always present,
Through every season
and every
circumstance.*

*As fresh
as the morning dew,
as **strong** as the eagle's wings,
as **precious** as a new-born baby.
Real.
Whole.
A Gift
To His beloved child.*

A Rainbow called HOPE – Part 1

No rain – no rainbows. Rainbows are God's promises <u>underlined</u>

My husband, my son and I were off on a little holiday—to a beautiful seaside spot on the coast of South Australia. We were all looking forward to the break. Unfortunately, the forecast for the weekend wasn't promising. Rain was on the horizon—lots of it. Storms, too. Rain by the sea wasn't my idea of a perfect time away. Although ... I have to admit that living in Australia has taught me what a blessing it is to have rain.

And so, as we looked forward to a happy weekend away, I even welcomed the rain, hugging the thought to myself that if rain was promised—perhaps we might even see a rainbow. As we drove down the Yorke Peninsula to our destination, the seaside village of Port Hughes, my heart quickened. I soon spotted what I was hoping for—an enchanting rainbow. It was a truly splendid splash of glory that adorned an overcast sky. I whipped out my camera and started clicking away as fast as I could.

About fifty clicks later, the rainbow was still smiling down at us. Talk of catching rainbows! I felt warmed by the love of a God who gave us this perfect rainbow at the very start of our holidays. We arrived at our destination and settled in quickly at a friendly and endearing caravan park. Deciding to enjoy a walk along the foreshore before dusk descended, I asked God to bless us with another rainbow—this time, one by the sea. I'd never seen one near the ocean!

Shan, Asela and I enjoyed a delightful ramble on a sparkling beach of soft sand, decked with ornate sea shells and long strands of emerald sea weed. We spotted a nice long pier, so of course we had to walk the length of it. When we reached the end of the pier, we turned back to gaze back at the shore. And then ... I saw it. A perfect rainbow spanned the sky, reaching right down to the seashore. My prayer had been answered. Thank you, Father.

My husband and I held hands and watched it. I heaved a deep, glad sigh of contentment. The rainbow's message was a sweet melody in my heart. *'God is faithful. God keeps His promises. I can trust Him.'* Our little break was an especially happy time and we returned refreshed and invigorated. Most of all, the knowledge of His faithfulness seeped into my being through the rainbow He gifted us with that day.

Did you know that with no rain, there would be no rainbows?

I'm sure you do, but I thought I'd mention it. It's so easy during the rainy seasons to forget the truth of that. But you know what? It *is* true. We need the rain. Farmers need the rain. Our gardens need the rain. The plants need the rain. And quite apart from that—a rainbow needs the rain so its beauty can burst forth! No rain, no rainbows!

There's a special rainbow: one called *hope*.

What does *hope* mean? To trust. To expect. To believe. To *not* give up.

'While there's life, there's hope.' Cicero

'Never lose hope.' *Polish Slogan*

'Once you choose hope, anything's possible.' Christopher Reeve

'When the world says, "Give up," Hope whispers, "Try it one more time."' *Unknown*

You and I sometimes need to wade through murky waters and get sopping wet in tropical storms as we journey through life. But God has not left us comfortless. He does shine a rainbow into our lives—especially when we need it most.

'Hope does not disappoint, because the love of God has been poured out within our hearts through the Holy Spirit who was given to us.' Romans 5:5 NASB

There was a time in my life when I crashed—and I clung onto a fine thread of hope. It seemed hardly present, because my pain was intense. But I knew from past experience that when I clung to the hope He offered me, He would come through for me again—as He had done so many many times before. Three months into the tough season, I was able to stand up again. Six months later—I was well on the way to being whole again. A year further on, I sat at a church service one morning, my heart overflowing with gratitude for the way He had come through for me. Jesus, my Hope, had been my strength and stay.

And so I can trust Him in other stormy seasons too, knowing that no matter how long the battle, I would eventually reach the mountain top of hope and healing and wholeness through Him who loves me.

A Rainbow called HOPE – Part 2

No rain – no rainbows. Rainbows are God's promises <u>underlined</u>

'But all shall be well,
And all shall be well,
And all manner of things shall be well...
He did not say, "You shall know no storms, no travails, no diseases.
He said "You shall not be overcome."'

Julian of Norwich

Yes, you shall not be overcome. The Word of God is filled with many wonderful promises and holds out many threads of hope—ones which will create a beautiful cross-stitch pattern out of your life. Right now, you might only see the underside of that design, but one glad day you will see the completed tapestry and gasp at its beauty.

'May the God of hope fill you with all joy and peace as you trust in Him, so that you may overflow with hope by the power of the Holy Spirit.'
Romans 15:13 NIV

Just as grieving is nature's way of recovery, I also believe that there also is a time for us to move on. I found five basic steps in the process of healing.

1. Acceptance

2. Trust

3. Nourishment

4. Practical Steps

5. Hope

One of the hardest things when a calamity hits is to accept what occurred. Once I'd planned to go and spend time with a sick friend. Months passed before I had the time to take the two-bus journey to her nursing home. I looked forward to brightening this precious friend's day. But to my shock and sadness, I found she'd just passed away. Too late! I kept berating myself. *What if I came last week? Why didn't I come earlier?* It was weeks before I let go of my guilt and sadness.

Often agreeing to the reality of a situation doesn't come easy. But the key to moving on is *acceptance*. That doesn't mean I condone any wrong done to me or others. God is on my case. I can trust Him. My part is simply to accept that the past cannot be altered. When I accept that I'm in the place I'm in, there's freedom. When I relinquish my desire to change the past, there is a new beginning. When I accept that God's ways are often different to mine, there is hope.

The second paver on the path to healing is *trust*. But ... how do you trust someone who lets you down? How do you trust God when you don't understand His ways?

'All I have seen teaches me to trust God for all I have not seen.'
Ralph Waldo Emerson

A baby is utterly dependent on his mum. He learns trust through her responses to his needs. When he cries, she comforts him. When he's hungry, she feeds him. When he's wet and uncomfortable, she changes his nappy. The baby learns that his mum is reliable. Our walk with God is much the same way.

The Christian life is no 100-metre dash—it is a moment-by-moment walk with the Lord. The more I get to know Jesus, the more my faith deepens. My own trust in God grew out of my friendship with Him. Over the years, as I encountered difficult seasons, He came through for me, over and over again. And so when the storms hit a new high—I knew I had Someone I could depend on.

So trust Him as the storm clouds deepen. Trust Him, because you know He is faithful. The pain will not subside immediately, but as you lean on Him—new murmurs of hope will stir within. And your pain will be changed slowly but surely into a season of hope and joy in the One who loves you deeply—and always will.

The third paver in a season of grief is *nourishment*. The chief nourishment for a Christian is of course the *Word of God*. A daily Quiet Time spent in solitude before God does wonders for a hurting soul. Make the Word your meat and drink, your bread and butter, your feast and wine. Delight in it. Claim every promise boldly. Believe what God says. Praise songs have often ministered to my troubled heart. Books that edify you are great sustenance. Nourishment might also arrive through loving affirming words spoken over you by family and friends.

What are the *practical steps* needed to overcome your season of grief? Later sections will deal with them. The 12 Umbrellas I mentioned back in the section *I need an umbrella!* are a good place to start.

The final stage of healing is the Rainbow whose Name is Jesus. He is the hope of all the world.

'We cannot always trace God's hand but we can always trust God's heart.'
Charles H. Spurgeon

We may not always understand what happens in our lives and why He allows it. But we can trust God wholly through the storms and through the rain. We can know with certainty that He will work it all out for good. We can journey with Him with a song in our hearts as we put on a cloak of thanksgiving and learn to dance in the rain.

Every Monday – Part 4

A little story in ten parts

When I told my friend Sue about the mysterious gifts that turned up every Monday, her eyes widened. 'Amazing! Why don't you try to find out who it could be? Don't you *want* to know?'

I shook my head. 'No, Sue. I don't want to find out. Perhaps it's one of the children. I don't want to spoil their fun.' I paused. 'Besides,' I added, 'I don't *want* to find out. It would burst my bubble, Sue. Do you know, I live from one Monday to the next. That's how I've got through the days and weeks since Peter died. It will be six months next week. I pretend sometimes that he's still alive. It keeps me going. I know it's not true, Sue. But when Monday comes, I have this curious feeling inside of me that he hasn't died after all and I don't want to lose it. It's as if nothing has changed, when in actual fact everything has. No—I don't want to know.' I hoped she would understand.

Sue's piercing blue eyes gazed towards me with care and concern and friendship. She hugged me. I struggled to keep my composure. I wiped the tears as they trickled down my cheeks. When would I ever get over it? How could I ever get over it? Did I even *want* to get over it? Peter had died in spring. Very ironic. Spring was a time of new growth. But my life had died that spring. How hard it would be for me to face each spring now.

Spring gave way to summer; and summer deepened into autumn. Winter was especially hard because winter was Pete's favourite season. He loved the cold; I hated it. He loved the winters. I enjoyed the summers. He and I were as different as chalk and cheese. But we fitted each other like a well-worn glove fitted one's hand—soft and comfortable. Just right. We were a team. We *had* been a team that is, I mentally corrected myself. Now the team had lost its leader.

... to be continued

Anne's Story

Friends' Stories 4

Having reached the ripe old age of 85, I thought I'd navigated many perilous seas and arrived at a safe harbour. I was settled, thinking I would remain at anchor for the rest of my days. Not so.

One day several years ago, I made a tough discovery. I found a lump in my left breast. I was shaken. Tests revealed it was malignant and the dreaded C word was pronounced. In a short time I was in hospital, having a total mastectomy and the removal of my lymph nodes, two of which were infected. It caught me off-guard at a time I least expected it.

But ... there were good things happened as a result. My eldest daughter, an oncologist in private practice in the United States flew to Sri Lanka to be with me. I didn't suffer even a twinge of pain and the whole experience felt unreal. I came home on the fourth day after surgery. Surprisingly, I even felt well enough to come to the computer to send a message of reassurance to my family and friends.

Ten days after that, with my surgeon's blessing, I travelled to Kandy, a city 120 kilometres away. Just a few days after that I was able to sit through six solid hours of the University's General Convocation. Perhaps it helped that my granddaughter was among the graduands. Not what one would expect after undergoing such surgery at the age of 85. I was blessed.

My eighty-sixth year turned out to be a real adventure. I started to have sudden, momentary blackouts. It was a deep concern, because I could fall down without warning and hurt myself further. On investigation, it was found to be caused by an irregular heartbeat. So I had another operation to install a pacemaker. And guess what! That wasn't all. It was discovered I was suffering from congestive heart failure. *Whew*!

In my view, the poet Browning was way off the mark when he wrote those much quoted lines: '*Grow old along with me; the best is yet to be.*' For most of us, all sorts of disabilities surface. Limbs don't function as they should, joints become arthritic, mobility is impaired, eyes grow dim, there is hearing loss, teeth fall out, so does hair, memory fails, the speed of change all around becomes bewildering. Loneliness sets in.

Yes, the rains do arrive—and drench me, time and time again. But God has blessed me and has brought me through each rainy season. There is one Source of strength we can depend on to the end of our days when we have built our house upon a rock instead of on shifting sands. Even if the rains come down and the floods rise up, we have a security that no power on earth can destroy.

When I went through my cancer journey, my doctor daughter's presence gave me strength. Through her, I felt the grace and presence of God. When my human flesh failed me, God's grace through human relationships kept me going. Four years later I am still alive and enjoying life, focussing on all that's good and feel more blessed every day. Yes, the rains of life have fallen in my life many times.

But God has always brought me through.

There was a time

My Stories – Four

I wheeled my loaded trolley to the car park, and a light drizzle dripped onto my shoulders. It was winter. It was grey. Wet. But I didn't mind. *I didn't mind at all.*

There was a time when even a few drops of rain bothered me. In the 'bad old days' I hadn't liked getting wet. I hadn't liked my hair looking like rain-drenched crow's feathers. I hadn't enjoyed the discomfort of feeling uncomfortably cold in damp clothes. I hadn't liked seeing grey rather than bright golden sunshine.

But eighteen beautiful years in this beautiful country have done me yeoman service—I've been helped in time of need. Many precious joys have been heaped upon my migrant head. Colombo, Sri Lanka, the country where I grew up had essentially only two types of weather—hot and humid or monsoonal downpours. Nothing in between. So when I was new to this land Down Under, I couldn't figure out why people spoke so glowingly of rain. One of my friends would email: *'Isn't the rain wonderful?'* or *'Aren't you enjoying this weather?'* and it would surprise me.

'How could anyone enjoy the greyness of rainy days?' I wondered. But not anymore. As the months turned into years, I experienced first-hand Australian droughts. As I slowly became Australian, weather-sensitivity grew in me. I found myself cheering when the rainy days arrived. I could go for a walk and get a dusting of rain on my head. I began to love the sound of the rain pattering down.

And a good thing it was. A sunny winter's day in Oz seems to be a rarity. Yet those rainy grey winter days give me a deeper appreciation for the sunny ones. And that's not all. I like seeing the different colours in the sky. Watching rainbows appear at random. Noticing streaks of sunlight appear under drab skies; or hearing the soft pelt of rain and the louder pings of hailstones clattering down.

There was a time when difficulties in my life made me feel bad inside. Now I might feel bad or sad or mad … depending on the circumstance. But I've changed my attitude because I see that my Master Designer is still at work. I know He is working out His kingdom and refining my character and using all that occurs in my life for good.

There was a time when rainy days had to be endured.

Now … I enjoy them.

There was a time when sad times in my life were perplexing.

Now … I may not always enjoy them—but I do know they have meaning and purpose.

And that for me is enough.

Little Nuggets 5

Nuggets to help me through those stormy seasons

Quotes that Bless

'The great love of God is an ocean without a bottom or a shore.'
C. H. Spurgeon

'In the centre of the hurricane there is absolute quiet and peace. There is no safer place than in the centre of the will of God.'
Corrie ten Boom

'Enjoy the little things, for one day you may look back and realise they were the big things.'
Robert Brault

'For peace of mind, resign as general manager of the Universe.'
Unknown

'Blessed is the man who is too busy to worry in the daytime and too sleepy to worry at night.'
Unknown

'Hope itself is like a star— not to be seen in the sunshine of prosperity, and only to be discovered in the night of adversity.'
Charles H. Spurgeon

'Giving up doesn't always mean you are weak. Sometimes

it means that you are strong enough to let go.'

Unknown

*'There is a place of quiet rest; there is a place of
comfort sweet, near to the heart of God.'*

Cleland B. McAfee

'You don't need to cry very loud. He is nearer to us than you think.'

Brother Lawrence

'Sometimes the best way to hold onto something is to let it go.'

Unknown

*'The greatest honour we can give the Almighty God is to
live gladly because of the knowledge of His love.'*

Julian of Norwich

Here's one to challenge you:

*'Life is too short to nurse one's misery. Hurry across the lowlands
so that you may spend more time on the mountain tops.'*

Phillip Brooks

And finally, one to nourish your soul:

*'Your emptiness is but the preparation for your being filled, and
your casting down is but the making ready for your lifting up.'*

Charles H. Spurgeon

The Centre of Your Will

Poem 5

Father God,
I am your Child
and
You are my loving
Father.

I come today
like a little girl
who
needs the comfort
of her Daddy's lap
His lavish embrace
His arms around her,
to
face
the world
with all that
it holds
for her.

Be my Rock,

my Guide,
my Hiding Place.

Oh Lord,
Be my Papa God
Whose arms
will never let me go.

I will stay here,
secure and
fearless,
knowing
that there is
nowhere safer than
the centre of Your will.

Nowhere better
to be
than by your side.
Kept
and nurtured
by You.

Splashing through the puddles – Part 1

Hanging onto a loving God; clinging onto HOPE

My son often revelled in mud puddles when he was little. No matter that I frowned as I watched his clean shoes and sparkling white socks become covered in mud, my boy's instinct was to jump into puddles. He did it with gusto. He was a little boy, after all.

There are times in life when we have no choice but to splash through puddles after rain. The puddles don't dry overnight. And so—we have to hitch up our skirts or trousers, ignore the murky water and continue splashing our way along a miry path.

Yet how do navigate through a puddle-filled universe? Let me share a few ways that helped me. First and foremost, I clung onto a loving God. His love helped to steer me through the darkness. Have *you* known that love? I found His love many many years ago, when as a sixteen-year-old I asked Jesus to be the mainspring of my existence and to steer my ship through all of life. Truly, once I discovered all Jesus had done for me, there was no other response I could make. *If He had died for me, what else could I do but live for Him?*

There were no fireworks then. But slowly and surely I started an incredible new journey. Saved not because of my goodness but simply because of His love. Saved by grace alone. What is 'grace'? The Undeserved Goodness of God in Christ Jesus. It was also an expedition of learning to do life in a brand new way. A fantastic, fabulous, thrilling voyage with Jesus as my

Leader and with the Holy Spirit as my Counsellor and Guide, as well as God the Father as a Father above all Fathers. An exhilarating journey!

The death and resurrection of Jesus—God made flesh—gave me what I needed. I had a new start in life. Purpose. Identity as God's beloved child. A future bright with His promises. The assurance of life after death. A new Family—fellow believers as my brothers and sisters. Being able to join in with the marvellous story of God. What riches! All this changed the direction of my life.

Not that I always got it right, of course. There were valleys between the mountains and rain amidst the sunshine. I failed at times. But my Guide has been all He promised to be … and more. Through Jesus Christ, all God's promises have become a 'YES' for all time. Life holds meaning and purpose.

Years later when a big storm crashed into my life, I did have Someone to cling to and I made it through with His help. I began a journal called *'Listening to God'*. You see, for years, I had *tried* to listen to God. Now, I was given a profound opportunity to listen. I reflected deeply on each word I read in His Word. Every status on Facebook that spoke from God's heart to mine, I copied into my journal. Every word of substance I read I took heed of. I listened to Him as never before.

And I believe I heard Him.

He whispered into my sad heart that He would never let me go. My time of grief turned into a season of pruning. It was painful. He showed me what my heart really looked like—murky and messy—a lot like a large, grubby mud puddle. Reflecting on the sin lurking inside wasn't easy: wrong attitudes needed changing, pride needed replacing with humility, mistaken ideas needed to be exchanged for right ones.

In the midst of His work in my life, He also showed me the extent of His amazing love. At last, after many years of following Jesus—I finally began to understand the magnitude of GRACE. I would never take God's grace for granted again. It was as if God said to me: *'See, Nushi. This is what the inside of your heart looks like.'* I didn't like what I saw. But He spoke in love. Not as an angry tyrant but a loving Father.

Not as a vengeful God, but a merciful Friend filled with compassion. He continued to do spring-cleaning in my life. He also assured me how much He loved me *in spite* of every sin in my life. He told me that in Christ I had no condemnation. He taught me many lessons that season: lessons in humility … love … learning to live God's way.

A moment by moment walk with Him.

I finally learnt to truly give Him my all, to allow Him to increase in my life and myself to decrease. I was being taught how to be pure and blameless before Him. He showed me the vital responsibility I had to live a life that was truly His. A responsibility as a follower of Jesus. A responsibility as a Christian writer. A responsibility because I was His child and His witness to the world.

He reminded me that I could never point a finger at others because I too was a sinner saved through grace. He taught me that, if He forgave me all my sin, the least I could do was to forgive others. I got drenched and dirty as I splashed through those mud puddles. But His love cleansed me and His grace healed me. As I look back, I know now that my period of grief and of pruning was needed and one which reaped many rewards.

Splashing through the puddles – Part 2

Hanging onto a loving God; clinging onto HOPE

A verse from the gospel of John grabbed me one day. *'He cuts off every branch in Me that bears no fruit, while every branch that does bear fruit He prunes so that it will be even more fruitful.'* John 15:2 NIV

I'd read it before, but this time a light switched on in my mind. It brought me fresh hope, like sunshine following winter rain. I realised why I was being pruned. Not because God was angry with me—but because He loved me. What encouragement! My present season would usher in a beautiful new period of bearing more fruit for Jesus. I loved that.

It was something to hold during those dark days of grief. *'I will lead the blind by ways they have not known, along unfamiliar paths I will guide them; I will turn the darkness into light before them and make the rough places smooth. These are the things I will do; I will not forsake them.'* Isaiah 42:16 NIV

'Forget the former things; do not dwell on the past. See, I am doing a new thing! Now it springs up; do you not perceive it? I am making a way in the wilderness and streams in the wasteland.' Isaiah 43:18–19 NIV

I made sure that season that my self-talk blessed me. Many of us often talk to ourselves in a fashion we'd never dream of talking to another. *'You dope! What did you do that for?'* Or: *'I am an idiot,'* or *'Stupid me.'* Does that sound familiar?

Perhaps you had a Mum who criticised you often. Or a Dad who said you were to blame for what went wrong. A teacher who corrected you all the time. Or a sibling who had fun at your expense. Have you ever listened to your self-talk?

When I was learning to drive, I had an excellent instructor. Six years after getting my licence, I still hear his voice in my head. *'Follow the shape of the road and stop.' 'Check if clear, clear; then go.'* His voice in my head is a good one—and still helps me. But there are other voices we often hear from our past which may not be as positive.

I made sure during that season that I only spoke words to myself which brought wholeness and hope. I learnt to pat myself on the back even if no one else did. I whispered, *'Well done, Anusha,'* when I did something well, when I persevered or when I didn't give into discouragement. People around you may know what you are going through. So it's a good idea to cheer yourself on, especially when no one else does.

Another way that I splashed through the puddles was by telling myself that I would persevere *as long as it took.*

'Therefore, since we are surrounded by such a great cloud of witnesses, let us throw off everything that hinders and the sin that so easily entangles. And let us run with perseverance the race marked out for us, fixing our eyes on Jesus, the pioneer and perfecter of faith. For the joy set before Him He endured the cross, scorning its shame, and sat down at the right hand of the throne of God. Consider Him who endured such opposition from sinners, so that you will not grow weary and lose heart.' Hebrews 12:1–3 NIV

Perseverance. A long word for a long road. Please do determine to hang in there for as long as it takes. If I listened to my feelings, I would have given up. But the Word of God was like a light shining in the darkness. It reminded me that: *'No one has ever seen, no one has ever heard, no one has ever imagined what God has prepared for those who love him.'* 1 Corinthians 2:9 ERV

'And have you completely forgotten this word of encouragement that addresses you as a father addresses his son? It says, "My son, do not make light of the Lord's discipline and do not lose heart when He rebukes you, because the Lord disciplines the one he loves, and He chastens everyone He accepts as his son." Endure hardship as discipline; God is treating you as His children. For what children are not disciplined by their father?' Hebrews 12:5–7 NIV

Yes, my season of pruning was a blessing not a curse. God disciplined me not because he was punishing me, but because He loved me. The passage went on to tell me: *'No discipline seems pleasant at the time, but painful. Later on, however, it produces a harvest of righteousness and peace for those who have been trained by it. Therefore, strengthen your feeble arms and weak knees. "Make level paths for your feet," so that the lame may not be disabled, but rather healed.'* Hebrews 12:11–13 NIV

Finally, after several months, I found myself reaping a bountiful harvest of righteousness and peace following my season grief and pruning. What a blessing it was. And so I rejoiced. I shed tears again, but this time they were tears of thanksgiving. God's Word had proved true. His season of pruning in my life had brought me to a good place. I was a better person for my season of grief.

Don't believe what Satan tells you. One day you will be on the other side of this season, not mud-splattered, but washed clean through His love and grace, refreshed by His mercy and dressed in robes of righteousness.

'When life is heavy and hard to take, go off by yourself. Enter the silence. Bow in prayer. Don't ask questions. Wait for hope to appear. Don't run from trouble. Take it full-face. The "worst" is never the worst. Why? Because the Master won't ever walk out and fail to return. If he works severely, he also works tenderly. His stockpiles of loyal love are immense.' Lamentations 3:28–32 (The Message)

Keep clinging to Jesus.

'Courage doesn't always roar. Sometimes courage is the voice at the end of the day saying, "I will try again tomorrow."'

Mary Anne Radmacher

May you feel His love all around you today. Before you, beneath you, beside you, behind you, above you and around you. His love is your Hope and your Shield.

'Weeping may endure for a night, but joy comes in the morning.' Psalm 30:5 NKJV

Every Monday – Part 5

A little story in ten parts

I dreaded the first anniversary of Pete's death. *How could I bear it?* Re-living the months before his death was bad enough. June 16 was the day he'd been diagnosed with his brain tumour. I tried not to think about it, but the memories pushed their way into my mind—a bouncy dog determined to come to the forefront, begging for attention.

The dates danced before my eyes. June 28, the date of his operation. June 29, tiptoeing into the ICU to visit him, my heart right down in my heavy brown boots. June 30—when the doctor shook his head. I had known then that the miracle I'd hoped for would not happen. July 12—when Pete came home for a few days. What a special time that had been!

July 20, when he had to be rushed into emergency in the middle of the night because he couldn't breathe. July 29—some respite, when he and I sat close on the sofa, relishing our time together, because we knew our days were numbered. I could still picture his sweet boyish smile and his *'Come here, little girl.'* I recalled the warmth of his touch on my hand. In my mind's eye I could see again the impishness of his smile, I could smell the comforting scent of his after-shave lotion.

The final date etched in my mind was September 17—the day my husband and best friend had died. I wished I could go to sleep through the whole day so I would not have to dwell upon it. True, this past twelve months had seen me taking a few baby steps in recovery. I had actually laughed the previous night when my daughter-in-law Sonia told me something that little Keith had said. It felt disrespectful to Pete that I could laugh again. But I was sure Pete wouldn't mind. In fact, he would smile and say: '*Good on you, Lizzie girl. That's the spirit.*'

…to be continued

Lorraine's Story

Friends' Stories 5

I could share with you story after story of God's faithfulness in my life. However, let me share a recent experience. My usual job was in the food industry. I'd worked at one place for over fifteen months, and had tried hard to care for my co-workers and my customers and to please God through it. I'd made many great friends among the workers and the customers whom I served.

One day I came to work to be told by my boss: *'It's a quiet time now. We don't need you any more, Lorraine. You can leave.'*

What a shock, although … it was not entirely unexpected. My boss had initially given me lots of responsibility but, as time went on, seemed to dislike the fact I was popular and respected by others. No matter what I did—it was never enough for her.

When she asked me to leave, she refused to give a reason. I didn't argue or fight. I walked quietly to a table nearby and sat there for the rest of the day. It was the best thing I could have done. Many customers turned up, stunned to discover I was no longer a part of the establishment. I was acknowledged and affirmed. Some of them went away and came back with farewell gifts for me. It was an emotional time.

I knew God was pleased with me and it meant a lot to me. The added esteem and love of my customers was the icing on the cake and a great ending to my time of work at that workplace. However, being the sole wage earner in my family, I did need a steady income. So the problem was how to cope financially. Having time off work was actually a good thing. I had worked so hard for the past year I needed some time to relax, unwind, spend with God, catch up with friends, make my garden more presentable and smell a few roses.

Smelling roses was not part of my usual agenda—simply because I didn't have a moment to spare in my busy life. Perhaps this was a gift from God? Was He asking me to leave? If that was the case, I could accept it. And that would mean I wasn't really unfairly dismissed. God simply had no more need of my work there and was paving the way to a better life.

And so, midst of my turmoil and anger as well as sadness, I also had a deep joy welling up inside me. For the next few weeks, I trusted in my God—Jehovah Jireh—who has been my provider for many years. I went away for a few days to recover. Two friends gave me the use of their car filled with petrol. In quiet, beautiful surroundings and in the presence of God, I was renewed and rejuvenated. I returned three days later to find some other caring friends had paid for my stay. God was providing for me through them.

Many friends gave me money. How I appreciated their care! But … I was determined I would not use the money unless I needed it. I put it all into an envelope. When I went to the bank, I discovered to my surprise that I had … not 60 dollars, as I thought, but $460. I was speechless. I did some work cleaning houses so I could buy the daily bread for me and my son. I also enjoyed special moments relaxing and enjoying my new found freedom! It was wonderful. When I was tempted to worry about it, God reminded me He was looking after me. Exactly a month after I lost my job, I received a phone call letting me know I had a new job.

I had applied for about twenty positions but had no calls for an interview. But one Sunday, about three weeks after I lost my job, I went to church only to meet someone who had an opening available for me. That had to be a God thing. I'd actually asked Him for four weeks annual leave just before I lost my job. He had blessed me with exactly that. I had four weeks to do as I pleased.

As I look back, my heart is filled with awe. You see, I don't know how God did it, but He did. He looked after me for that one month I didn't have any income. My purse *always* had enough for my needs. I can't account for it. I didn't even need to touch the money that my friends gave me. God provided for me. He gave me a month's holiday—one which I badly needed. And then He brought the right job for to me, so I could serve Him again as well as have sufficient to live on.

I was down to my last $25 dollars with two whole weeks left till pay day when my Uncle Bill phoned me from Canada. He told me he'd put in some money into my account. I found $1000 the next time I checked. Yes, God provided for me once again—this time through my beloved Uncle Bill. Finally, I'd like to quote the words of Joseph: *'You intended to harm me, but God intended it for good to accomplish what is now being done, the saving of many lives.'* Genesis 50:20 NIV

My story is different to Joseph's story, but there is one factor in both our stories that are similar. Other people may try to hurt us. But when we walk in God's ways, any harm intended for us only turns into good. Hard times become good times. Pain turns into praise. Heartache and uncertainty into joy and security.

All praise to our awesome God!

Winter of Rich Content

My Stories – Five

I was walking to a nearby shopping centre to post a letter. I donned my winter jacket, put on my sneakers and was off. First I went to our neighbourhood oval and did two laps. I drank in the scenery of the hills, the view of the sea, the twinkling lights as they flickered on all around me.

I had to pass through the Rose Garden to reach the shopping centre. As I approached, I found that bands of orange tape covered the entrance. It was under renovation so I was forced to use a different path. I tried going down the next set of steps, but found to my dismay that it too was cordoned off. Oh dear. Change of Plan B to Plan C. It looked like a major repair of the Rose Garden was underway.

I found yet another path the shops. My dismay over the loss of my planned walk was blanketed by gratitude that there were many roads leading where I wanted to go. I glanced back at the Rose Garden. And then wandered back mentally on the season that I'd just passed through.

Just as I'd made several detours on my walk, I'd made lots of detours in my life that autumn. I had reached winter. Safely. I was content. The walk had not been on planned pathways. It had often been on rocky, uneven ground. I'd experienced a few months of difficulty and pain. I had had to take unusual trails, all new territory to me. But God had stepped in had led me along different walkways and brought me safely through.

It could have well been my winter of discontent. But no, the detours had brought rich blessing. God had revealed Himself afresh to me. He had changed me as I clambered down unfamiliar pathways and craggy rocks. He had brought me safely to the other side.

And when winter came? Yes, the season was golden and I enjoyed it. I had arrived in my *Winter of Rich Content*.

Little Nuggets 6

Nuggets to help me through those stormy seasons

Psalm 34 NIV

1. I will extol the Lord at all times; His praise will always be on my lips.

    Father, I will praise you today and every day. Even when life hurts.

2. I will glory in the Lord; let the afflicted hear and rejoice.

    I will boast in You, Father. Use my words to bless others.

3. Glorify the Lord with me; let us exalt His name together.

    I will call others too to lift You high, Lord Jesus.

4. I sought the Lord, and He answered me; He delivered me from all my fears.

    Thank You for the many times You have helped me, Lord.

5. Those who look to Him are radiant; their faces are never covered with shame.

    I stay close to You, Jesus. Thank You for Your promises.

6. This poor woman called, and the Lord heard him; He saved him out of all his troubles.

    Thank You, God. Please save me again. I need You.

7. **The angel of the Lord encamps around those who fear Him, and He delivers them.**

   Thank You that You will do this for me today. I wait on You, Lord.

8. **Taste and see that the Lord is good; blessed is the one who takes refuge in Him.**

   I choose to take refuge in You today, Father.

9. **Fear the Lord, you His holy people, for those who fear Him lack nothing.**

   Help me remember, Father, that I have all I need.

10. **The lions may grow weak and hungry, but those who seek the Lord lack no good thing.**

    Help me believe it, Lord. Thank You that I lack no good thing because You will care for me.

11. **Come, my children, listen to me; I will teach you the fear of the Lord.**

    I am listening, Lord.

12. **Whoever of you loves life and desires to see many good days,**

13. **keep your tongue from evil and your lips from telling lies.**

    Help me guard my tongue and speak Your words, Lord.

14. **Turn from evil and do good; seek peace and pursue it.**

    I choose the way of integrity, Lord. I will seek Your peace.

15. **The eyes of the Lord are on the righteous and His ears are attentive to their cry;**

    I know You hear me, Lord. I know You will answer.

16. but the face of the Lord is against those who do evil, to cut off the memory of them from the earth.

    Help me not sin as I go through my season of grief.

17. The righteous cry out, and the Lord hears them; He delivers them from all their troubles.

    That's so comforting to hear, Lord. Not one or two troubles—but ALL.

18. The Lord is close to the broken-hearted and saves those who are crushed in spirit.

    Come near me, Lord. I am crushed in spirit. I know You will lift me up and bring deliverance at the right time.

19. A righteous person may have many troubles, but the Lord delivers him from them all

    All of it, Lord? Thank You, Jesus. I wait upon You.

20. He protects all his bones, not one of them will be broken.

    I am safe in Your care, Lord. *Thank You so very much.*

21. Evil will slay the wicked; the foes of the righteous will be condemned.

    Justice is Your department, Lord. So I will not worry about those who have done me wrong. I will allow You to handle it.

22. The Lord will rescue His servants; no one who takes refuge in Him. will be condemned.

    Lord, you are my Helper. I take refuge under the shadow of Your wings.

God will....

1. Deliver me from my fears
2. Make my face radiant
3. Take away my shame
4. Send His angel to encamp around me and to deliver me
5. Bless me when I take refuge in Him
6. Give me all I need
7. Listen and hear me when I cry to Him
8. Deliver me from all my troubles
9. Stay close to me when I am broken-hearted
10. Save me and protect my bones—none will be broken

He will....

1. Never condemn me
2. Be my Refuge

What must I do?

1. Extol and praise Him *always* through every circumstance
2. Glorify Him
3. Seek Him
4. Look to Him
5. Call out to Him
6. Taste Him and find His goodness
7. Take refuge in Him
8. Fear Him
9. Speak only the truth
10. Turn from Evil
11. Do good
12. Seek and pursue peace

There are times

Poem 6

There are times
in our lives
When time stands still
The world stops turning
And we stand
Bewildered
At the hand that life's cards have dealt us.

Times,
When the sure foundation under us
Rocks
And crashes down
And we falter
And slip
Into the cracks
Not feeling
We could get up again!

There are times
In my life
When I hurt,

And keep hurting.
Reeling
from all that
life has
thrown my way.

Those are times
I run
To the Master
With my heart
feeling squeezed
And tight
And dry
Emotions
all stolen
Except
the one of Despair
Sadness
Not knowing
How I could face
tomorrow.

Those are times
When my Master
comes
He wraps
me in His love.
He tells me
that
He loves me.

He will hold
me fast
And not let me go
today,
tomorrow
or ever.

Because
no matter what happens.

I remain,
Always His.

Laughter, the Best Medicine – Part 1

Finding Joy and Hope amidst those rainy seasons

I'd been getting drenched in a rainy season and I wasn't coping. So I did what the doctor ordered—I turned to a caring friend for help. I shared a bit of my story with her, tears close to the surface. I shared, she listened. Her understanding and empathy blessed me beyond measure. Her words comforted me. Her prayers brought solace to my troubled heart.

I had even managed not to cry. Quite an accomplishment seeing how fragile I was. Over the next four months, I turned to her for her listening ears and her prayers another five or six times. Each time I left her, I was refreshed. We laughed a lot together. And ... that laughter was the medicine I needed. For the first time in my life I saw the healing power of laughter.

Many books on health and mental health re-iterate this truth: laughter is very good for us. Sick patients are encouraged to watch funny movies, because laughter aids their recovery. Endorphins are released when we laugh and they are natural pain-killers.

Yet when we're in deep pain, laughing doesn't occur easily. My wise friend had the amazing ability to bring humour into our interactions. No wonder I felt better for spending half an hour with her. That humour was my lifeline.

Smiling is also deeply beneficial. No matter how we feel, if we force our mouths to smile, we feel better. And so, during times I've felt down or depressed, I have tried this remedy. And yes, I'm happy to say it does work.

So a good technique for reaching the restorative calm and peace during troubled times is making your mouth do what it doesn't want to do. *Smile*. Every time you go into your bedroom or bathroom, look at the mirror and smile. Smile because it's medicine. Smile because it will help you heal. And take my word for it—it works. Recently, I heard of a way you could do this effortlessly, by sticking a pen between your teeth and keeping it there for a bit. Would you like to try that?

Laughing is even better. Borrow several funny movies and work your way through them. Laugh all you like—it's good for you. Perhaps you could seek the company of friends with a good sense of humour and spend some time listening to their jokes. Laugh at them. I'd like to share a secret. I often find healing through my tears. When I cry, all the toxins locked inside me must leave my system, because I usually become lighter and happier afterwards. Surprisingly, laughter does the same.

'The more things we can laugh about, the more alive we become. The more things we can laugh about together, the more connected we become.' Frank Pittman

It's true. Laughter connects people together in amazing ways. My husband has a great sense of humour—one of the many reasons I married him! 33 years since we forged our life-long relationship—we still find plenty to laugh about. It's a natural energiser which keeps our relationship fresh and alive. I've often felt a special bond with strangers when I've connected with them through humour. So laughter not only lightens my load in painful moments; it also brings me closer to others. What a great tonic—a free, God-given one at that.

God has a great sense of humour, don't you think? He made the Ant and the Antelope, the Mouse and the Mammoth. His creation is filled with all things bright beautiful and even downright funny. The amazing sea creatures in the depths of the ocean. The pesky fly that refuses to leave you alone. The mosquito that drives you crazy by buzzing incessantly in your ear. God made all things good. He made all things enormous. He made all things small. He made you and me. Where does our sense of humour come from, but from our Creator Himself?

And what of celebrations? How can we celebrate when the world is grey and life doesn't seem worth living? Of course it isn't easy, but we can try. Celebrate the person you are. Celebrate the accomplishment of getting through another day. Celebrate the people in your life who have added to it. Sometimes there is no reason to celebrate. Sometimes, there is only grief … and pain… and tears.

Sometimes laughter might feel like a betrayal of a loved one who has died. But celebration doesn't have to be about partying. When a loved one dies, you can celebrate all that she or he meant to you. Write a letter thanking her for the great times you shared together. Call a friend and share the precious memories you have of her. Celebrate his unique ways. Celebrate the accomplishments in his life. Make a photo-book with pictures of your loved one and recall the cherished times you spent together. It might bring more tears than smiles. It might mean more pain for a time. But it also means that you remember all the good times and realise it was worth it.

Celebrating her might mean writing a story about her or an appreciation to the newspapers. If you are good with your paintbrush, perhaps you could paint a picture of him. Maybe you could pull out all the photographs you have of him and make a collage of them? Perhaps you could compose a song about her?

Celebrating may be also doing a good deed in memory of your loved one. Helping in a soup kitchen? Giving away meals to the homeless? Visiting an orphanage and spending time with children? Taking gifts to an old people's home and listening to other lonely people? Yes, the potential for celebrations are endless. And helping others as a way of remembering your loved one means that many others would benefit in the process.

Laughter, the Best Medicine – Part 2

Finding Joy and Hope amidst those rainy seasons

When Jesus died, the last thing on his disciples' minds would have been a celebration of any kind. They had witnessed the death of their Master. Their hopes were crushed. Their hero was gone—the One they pinned their hopes on. *Where was God in all of this?*

Though the disciples didn't know it at the time, Good Friday wasn't the end of the story. It may have been the end of one chapter but it was the grand start of another—the most important chapter of all. *Jesus rose from the dead.*

The Christian narrative resounds with hope and joy. It's been called *the Great Reversal*. In the kingdom of God—the last shall be first. The foolish are the wise. The weak are the strong. The leaders are servants. The meek inherit the earth. Death is defeated and is the doorway to life. Sorrow is turned to triumph. C.S. Lewis paints the picture for us beautifully in *The Chronicles of Narnia*: *'Winter began stirring backward.'*

The interesting truth is that Christ's coming didn't take away the natural order of things. The Great Reversal was actually the beginning of a restoration planned since the beginning of time.

Isaiah 11:6–9 NIV is a passage that resonates with hope.

'The wolf will live with the lamb, the leopard will lie down with the goat, the calf and the lion and the yearling together; and a little child will lead them. The

cow will feed with the bear, their young will lie down together, and the lion will eat straw like the ox. The infant will play near the hole of the cobra, and the young child put his hand into the viper's nest. They will neither harm nor destroy on all My holy mountain, for the earth will be full of the knowledge of the Lord as the waters cover the sea.'

Isaiah later shares a few more joys we may anticipate.

'The Sovereign Lord will wipe away the tears from all faces; He will remove the His people's disgrace from all the earth. The Lord has spoken. In that day they will say, "Surely this is our God; we trusted in Him, and He saved us. This is the Lord, we trusted in Him; let us rejoice and be glad in His salvation.'
Isaiah 25:8–9 NIV

And so our rainy days are tinged with hope of better things to come. The Christian perspective is different to the world's take on life. We have Someone who is in control even when it seems otherwise. We know that God works for the good of all who love Him—through every circumstance. We know that tragedy isn't what it seems to be. That the *now* is not the end of the story—it's only a brief moment in time. We know also that, for Christians, the End of the Story is one that resonates with bright hope—a hope that will not disappoint us.

The difficult part is clinging onto that hope when the boat is sinking, the lightning is flashing across the sky and thunder booming so loud we can't hear the music. Our minds might know the truth but transferring it to our emotions and feelings isn't easy.

How do we do that? Here's my answer. *Simply look to Jesus.*

'God, who got you started in this spiritual adventure, shares with us the life of His Son and our Master Jesus. He will never give up on you. Never forget that.'
1 Corinthians 1:9 (The Message)

Hang in there for as long as it takes—just one day, one hour, one moment at a time. Smiling and laughing when possible—despite your pain—will help you feel better. Believing that brighter days are ahead is important. A hymn by Anna Waring who lived in the nineteenth century has blessed me often through many stormy seasons.

> *'In heavenly love abiding, no change my heart shall fear.*
> *And safe in such confiding, for nothing changes here.*
> *The storm may roar without me, my heart may low be laid,*
> *But God is round about me, and can I be dismayed?*
>
> *Wherever He may guide me, no want shall turn me back.*
> *My Shepherd is beside me, and nothing can I lack.*
> *His wisdom ever waking, His sight is never dim.*
> *He knows the way He's taking, and I will walk with Him.*
>
> *Green pastures are before me, which yet I have not seen.*
> *Bright skies will soon be over me, where darkest clouds have been.*
> *My hope I cannot measure, my path to life is free.*
> *My Saviour has my treasure, and He will walk with me.'*

Anna L. Waring

Seasons pass. The winter disappeared in greener pastures and lush meadows to walk in and to enjoy. My hope was one that could not be bound or measured. My Saviour who was and is my deepest Treasure walked every step of the way with me in all kinds of weather. He held me as we splashed together in the rain. May you find comfort as you hope for brighter seasons.

When life gives you a rainy day, play in the mud puddles.

Will you join me?

Every Monday – Part 6

A little story in ten parts

I had used our lovely large tea chest from China to store all my Monday gems. Forty-eight Mondays had come and gone and each Monday had brought me a fresh treasure. Some of them were little gifts—a postcard, a pen, even a thimble. One Monday there was a newspaper cutting dated 21 August, 2000. That was a write-up about the orchestra—the orchestra Peter had played in for 25 years. How I cherished the photograph, even though it was a little difficult to spot Peter in it—he was in the back row, sitting next to the other bassoonist.

On days when I felt extra lonesome, I would bring my little wooden stool to the guestroom and sit near the tea chest. I'd put on Peter's favourite music; his Simon-and-Garfunkel CD. I'd wear his much loved sweater—a soft dark brown one which had large black and white criss-cross markings on it. Even though it was far too large for me, I felt he was close to me when I wore it.

I would go through the chest, picking up the gifts one by one and fingering them. Perhaps it was strange that I didn't try to find out who sent them. I was too sad, too tired and too heartsick to try. I just enjoyed discovering what each Monday brought me. Twelve months of Mondays had brought my Peter back to life in a strange way. His death was more bearable because of those treasures. And so I chose to ignore the warning signals which my mind urgently whispered in my ear. *Would the gifts stop one day? How would I cope then?* I didn't listen to the sensible voice in my head. *How could I?*

… to be continued

Valerie's Story – All the Days of My life

Friends Stories 6

I sat by Richard's bedside in Intensive Care in a state of shock. My strong healthy husband was under a sentence of death. Just over a week ago, he had seemed to be fine.

The only reason he consented to see a doctor was that he had an episode of pain while waiting for me at the surgery. I'd insisted he made an appointment to have it checked out. The doctor examined him and said he probably had an ulcer—but would send him to see a specialist to be sure. Later Richard told me he had a 'gut feeling' something was wrong.

The specialist was sure it was a treatable ulcer, especially since Richard had experienced no other episode. However, because our GP had requested it, he arranged for Richard to have an endoscopy. That endoscopy changed our lives. What a huge shock! It revealed Richard had stage four stomach cancer. Within a couple of days, Richard was operated on and his stomach removed, to 'buy him a bit more time'.

I watched him lying there—tubes coming out of him seemingly from everywhere. He had oxygen to help him breathe, drips to distribute fluids and medication. His pallor was deathly white. I was shattered.

But into my mind dropped a verse from Psalm 23: *'Surely goodness and mercy shall follow me all the days of my life.'*

All at once, I was filled with a great anger toward God. 'What is good and merciful about this?' I cried out to Him.

God's gentle voice spoke into my heart. 'What I am saying is that, no matter what your circumstances, My goodness and mercy will be with you all the days of your life.'

Immediately, my heart was flooded with peace. This peace remained with me through the difficult weeks and months ahead.

A few months later my beloved Richard died. It was not an easy time. There was great pain and sorrow but, in some inexplicable way, there was also joy and laughter. That was eleven years ago. I have spent a great many of those years 'walking in the valley'. Six months after Richard's death, I was diagnosed with cancer in my right breast. While undergoing treatment, I was diagnosed with a kidney problem which needed surgery. Other medical conditions arose. Asthma, heart problems—which affected my diabetes. I became insulin-dependent, then had yet another occurrence of breast cancer, this time in my left breast. I had had several bad falls, resulting in broken bones.

'How much more can you take?' I have been asked. Thankfully, I have been able to share with my friends of the times when I have been filled with such joy I could hardly contain it. Along with the joy, there is the absolute assurance of my Heavenly Father's goodness and mercy following me all the days of my life.

The Bag

My Stories – Six

I was at my volunteer job at my church. I felt unusually sleepy that day, so I was looking forward to getting home for a read and rest in bed. I gathered my belongings—my books, water bottle, glasses, phone. I stuffed them into my bag and shut down my computer. I made sure the door to the storeroom was locked and tidied the office.

I loved working at the church, meeting clients and doing my mite for the Kingdom. Locking the main door, I headed off to my car. I glanced down at the carrier bag in one hand. And at the water bottle in the other. Something was missing. Something important. *My handbag.* Where was it?

I ran back, unlocked the door and retrieved my bag from under my desk. I wouldn't have got far without it since my car keys were in it. My bag's one of my most prized possessions: it contains my house keys, my car keys, my work keys, my purse, my money, my credit cards. My glasses.

I wouldn't mind losing a number of my possessions, but not my hand bag.

Every experience in life affords me a treasured gift if I allow it to. It is up to me to find it, take it and use it.

Life experiences are learning experiences. Sad times, troubled times, bad times, times of heartache, times of pain are ideal learning places and growing grounds. How foolish I would be if I walk away from any moment leaving its treasures behind. It would be a bit like walking out the door of CareLink that day—ignoring the loss of such an important possession.

What can I take with me from this rainy season in my life?

Little Nuggets 7

Nuggets to help me through those Stormy Seasons

Attitude – My Friend in Times of Grief

What are some of the *attitudes* I can choose today?

1. God loves me. Always. No matter what. No matter if I am sad. No matter what I have done. No matter if life is difficult. No matter if the world has stopped turning. Jesus loves me deeply. I shall rejoice and bask in His love for me.

2. God's GRACE is real. It is enough. I will lay hold of it today.

3. I will accept what I cannot change. I will change what I can. I will ask Him to show me which is which.

4. Life is sometimes painful. But God is FAITHFUL.

5. No matter what happens to me—my *attitude* is something that is always under my control. And so, in God's strength I shall wear the right *attitude* today.

6. God will carry me through. I will trust Him. Today. Tomorrow. Every day.

7. God permitted this season in my life for my good. I don't see it right now, but I will cling to that knowledge.

8. I'm struggling today, but better times are ahead. I will hold fast to Jesus.

9. I will choose to believe what I read in the Word about God. I will take hold of every promise in it.

10. I have many riches. I will take them as He offers them to me. Love, Freedom, Life, Warmth, Forgiveness, Grace, Power, Love, Joy, Strength, Peace. Hope.

Your Way, O Lord

Poem 7

Today I ask
That You
would walk with
me.

And though the storm
may rage,
Your Hand
will hold me,
Your love
will guide me,
Your light
will shine
in the darkness,
to show me
the way,
as it lights
my darkened path.

Today, I know not
What or where or why or how

But this I know for sure.
You who made me
You who called me
You who loved me
You who died for me
are still
able
to perform
all
that's needed
to make
my
life
Beautiful,
Full
and
Perfect.
Fashioned by You
for your purpose
and Your
Kingdom.

Tall Stories about Rainy Days – Part 1

The rain won't last forever. Hope dispels those rainy day myths

Modern men and women are bombarded by myths every day and every hour. Television commercials squawk at us that life is all about looking good and accumulating possessions. Old age doesn't seem to be the right destination. But then, is an early death preferable? For our lives to have value, do we need to stay eternally young? Often people project to society their most important yardstick in life: a well-paying job, a luxurious home, a respectable life. But is that what it's all about?

In the matter of grief, many myths and tall stories also abound. Which do we believe? Our beliefs shape us. My beliefs shape my lifestyle. When rainy days come my way, negative thoughts might overwhelm me, like the froth of waves on a windswept seashore. Frivolous myths are like that froth. Let's look underneath to find the golden grains of common sense just below the surface.

Rainy Day Myth #1:
God doesn't care for me. Otherwise He would not let me suffer so much.

There've been seasons in my life when I've wondered where God was and what He was doing. When my son was little, I longed to have another child. As we tried to conceive, it was not easy to watch my friends delight in their second or third child while God seemed to say 'No' to my request. But no matter how much I beseeched Him—nothing happened. Where was God? Why didn't He answer? Didn't He love me? There were other times when one of my family was sick and my prayers didn't seem to be answered. I knew God loved us. I knew He had power to help us. I knew He could do anything for me the moment I asked it … *so why didn't He?*

Once when I turned to God in confusion, He didn't give me an answer. Instead, He presented me with a verse from Scripture. *'Trust in the Lord with all your heart and lean not on your own understanding. In all your ways submit to Him, and He will make your paths straight.'* Proverbs 3:5–6 NIV

The *'lean not on your own understanding'* spoke to me powerfully. The thing was that, if I could have understood what was happening, I could have coped far better. But God didn't say: 'Trust Me and I will explain all.' He said instead: *'Trust Me with every fibre of your being. Don't try to decipher what's going on. Simply lean on Me. Allow Me to lead you all the way. I will lead you in the best path possible. Trust Me, My beloved child.'*

Ever since God spoke to me through that verse, I've tried to do less *'seeking to understand'* and more *trusting*. Sometimes I've failed—I could trust Him mentally, being aware that He was leading me, but emotionally I'd tremble. There have been other times, though, when I was able to stop fretting. I've said to Him: *'Lord, this is Your problem, not mine. And so I shall trust You.'* How sweet the peace that filled me then and how gratifying it was when He provided His solutions to my needs in His own way and time.

The kind of question to ask, I believe, is this one: *'What should I do now, Lord?'*

The truth is that nothing can touch me without His permission. The bigger truth is that when I cling on tight to my loving God and ask Him to work out His purposes for me, those storms that crash around me can all be used for good.

'And we know that in all things God works for the good of those who love Him, who have been called according to His purpose.' Romans 8:28 NIV

Not in *some* things but in *all* things. Not individually but collectively, God will work it all out for my good and for yours. Do you wonder why God permitted your tragedies to occur? I have no answer to that.

God's love is never in doubt. May He reveal it to you afresh today and in the weeks ahead. *'See what great love the Father has lavished upon us, that we should be called children of God! And that is what we are!'* 1 John 3:1 NIV

Rainy Day Myth #2:
This season is permanent.

When bad times happen, I feel it will last forever. Those are the times I am tempted to give up. What is the point in persevering, if nothing will ever change?

Life's lessons over the years have reminded me that it's not just what occurs to me, but my perception of events that will change my life or predict its outcome. If I treat each difficulty as one more in a series of disasters, my hope sinks low, like a dog who's been reprimanded and whose tail stops wagging and head droops.

But … if I treat each tough circumstance with courage and dignity—realising that into all life a little rain will fall—and that it isn't permanent, well then, I might be like the frisky puppy who's scolded for chewing his master's slipper, who runs away but then … returns jaunty and bright-eyed, with yet another slipper in his mouth.

Rainy day Myth # 3:
What happens to me today affects the whole of my life

If I fall and break my leg, the accident will definitely affect most of my present life. But would breaking my leg affect my life forever? Probably not. I hope not. When a relationship breaks, when a loved one dies, when one is diagnosed with an incurable illness, yes, does life changes forever. Sometimes, life stinks. Big time.

But whether I allow it to affect all of my life or just the present is up to me. I can use my sad times to teach me, to grow me, to bring me to a better place. Or I could mourn what I lost for the rest of my life. The choice is mine.

Tall Stories about Rainy Days – Part 2

The rain won't last forever. Hope dispels those rainy day myths

'Trust in God, let nothing disturb you, let nothing frighten you; all things pass; God never changes. Patience achieves what it strives for. He who has God finds he lacks nothing, God alone suffices. Teresa of Avila, 1515–82

As you wait for the storm to pass, take comfort in the knowledge that, as sure as night follows day, your own season of grey clouds will give way to bright skies and dancing sunbeams.

Rainy Day Myth # 4:
You are doomed to an unhappy life

When things go wrong, I could perceive it as another addition to all that's gone wrong before. I have found it helpful to view each calamity that befalls me as just one individual situation, not a part of a series of mishaps that go on forever.

Suffering is part of the sinful world we have been born into. When Adam and Eve sinned, sin entered the world. Suffering will continue to be part of our lot till we die. But Satan is a defeated foe. *'Keep a cool head. Stay alert. The Devil is poised to pounce, and would like nothing better than to catch you napping. Keep your guard up. You're not the only ones plunged into these hard times. It's the same with Christians all over the world. So keep a firm grip on the faith. The suffering won't last forever. It won't be long before this generous God who has great plans for us in Christ—eternal and glorious plans they are!—will have you put together and on your feet for good. He gets the last word; yes, He does.* 1 Peter 5:8–9 (The Message)

Part of resisting Satan is to defy thoughts that plunge us deeper into the abyss. Each time something bad occurs, I can use it to become better or bitter. It is often tempting to wallow in self-pity, or to believe I am a victim, but I lose out when I do. If I label myself a victim, I won't have the power to change a situation. But if I *refuse* to be a victim, then I will find ways of rising again in spite of and after every difficult season.

Rainy Day Myth # 5:
Others have it better than me

'Be kinder than necessary for everyone you meet is fighting some kind of battle.'
Unknown

When you're in a difficult place, it's easy to be mistaken about the world around you. To imagine others have an easy life, to envy those who don't seem to have a care in the world, to indulge in a pity party because everyone else is having a good time and you aren't.

I remember once chatting with a few friends during a tough season which they knew nothing about. I told them that I sometimes fight self-pity by comparing myself to others who have it worse than I do, so I could think more positively. A friend immediately turned to me and said: *'You! Why should you feel sorry for yourself? You have an easy life.'* It hurt me and I almost burst into tears. Her thoughtless comment reminded me that we don't know the truth of other people's struggles. I realised that I needed to be sensitive to others who may be going through tough times unknown to me.

Instead of being a collector of hurts, I need to be a collector of joy. When good times come—it's a good idea to gather its joy inside my heart. It will bless me when the rain clouds form. When bad times arrive, look for the good around. You may not find it easily. But it is there. A beautiful sunset.

A butterfly that softly alights on your shoulder. A child's infectious laugh. A pet dog that nuzzles close to you. The music that touches your soul. The delicious meal your spouse has set before you. Memories which will bring you comfort. Yes, be a collector of joy. In every season. Then, when the rainy seasons happen—you will have a stock of joy within to comfort and bless you.

There are many rainy day myths running around. Shed them when the tough times arrive. Grab on instead to the Word, to good friends, to happy memories. Take a walk in the park. Laugh together with a friend. Believe that brighter days are on the horizon. Because God's love will never fail.

'No, in all these things we are more than conquerors through Him who loved us. For I am convinced that neither death nor life, neither angels nor demons, neither the present nor the future, nor any powers, neither height nor depth, nor anything else in all creation, will be able to separate us from the love of God that is in Christ Jesus our Lord.' Romans 8:37–39 NIV

Every Monday – Part 7

A little story in ten parts

I felt close to my husband when I looked inside the chest. His love fell over me like a soft mantle, as I fingered the gifts. True, they didn't come from him, but it didn't matter. I would remember the fun times we had in days of yore. The thimble reminded of the time I found a thimble in the Christmas pudding—we had been married only for one short year then. I hadn't been able to find it afterwards and had worried that I had swallowed it. How Pete had teased me about it! I smiled, remembering.

The pen was very similar to one I'd given him for his fiftieth birthday—a beautiful Parker pen. He'd told me it was one of the nicest gifts he'd ever received. The scarf was soft and silky and grey. *His* colour. It reminded me of his blue grey eyes. The little flag of Ireland reminded me of the last holiday we had spent in Dublin five years ago. Oh memories that bless and burn! My grandmother used to say it repeatedly. I said it to myself often those days.

On Monday September 10, I was making chicken soup for dinner when the doorbell rang. It was 4 pm. I walked to the door and opened it. Yes, there was the familiar something on the doormat. I bent down and picked the little parcel. It was very small, wrapped in a cheery wrapping paper and tied with a bright red ribbon. I undid the bow. Inside was a photograph. A photograph of Peter and myself. On the reverse of it was written: '*I will always love you!*' in Peter's unmistakable handwriting.

I stared at it. This had been taken on our 30th wedding anniversary. Who had put it there? How did they get it? I held the photograph close to my chest. I remembered our night out celebrating our thirty years together. The food in the restaurant had not been up to our expectations. Peter had turned a night gone badly into a fun night. How much we'd laughed together as we'd walked home in the rain. We'd had a fight later that night about something so small that I couldn't even bring to mind what it had been about. But we'd made up, before we turned the light off that night. It had been a good anniversary. Leaving another yet precious memory behind to cherish now.

I picked up the paper lying on the doormat. This one didn't say the usual 'Next Monday'. It said: *'Next Monday—the final gift.'*

The final gift? It echoed in my mind like the sound of mocking laughter bouncing off the walls. I had been given fifty-one gifts over the year and I didn't even know who was leaving them. And now … and now … they would stop!

I walked inside the house and I sat down. I stared glassy-eyed at the wall in front of me. Should I call Sue? No! It wouldn't help! No one would understand, not even Sue. It felt as if I was losing Peter all over again. It was then I realised how much I had relished waiting for Mondays. I'd kept my sanity because of each Monday and the hope it brought me. The unceasing pain in my heart seemed a bit more bearable ever since that first rose was laid on my door mat. No more Monday gifts. No more reminders of Peter. How would I get through it? The pain was a dagger in my heart.

How would I go on?

…to be continued

Gloria's Story

Friends' Stories 7

My husband Steve was terminally ill and we knew his time was running out. Our eldest son and his wife were expecting a baby and my husband badly wanted to be there for the birth. However, six months before the due date, God took my beloved husband home. It was a very sad time for me. I was supported by my church family who rallied around and helped in all sorts of ways, both practical and spiritual. I thanked God for them daily.

The baby turned out to be twins. Naturally, it was a time of great excitement for us as we awaited their birth. But suddenly … the bombshell dropped. We discovered that the boy twin was in trouble—he was getting smaller instead of bigger. The consultant told my son and his wife to let nature take its course. The baby would die in-utero, but they would have a full term healthy baby girl. They went home devastated. They phoned me to tell me the shocking news.

I suggested that we should pray about it. The next day they told me that they had decided to ask for a second opinion. They went to another Specialist who told them he was willing to deliver the twins by Emergency C-Section, but he could not promise that either baby would survive. The twins were born the following day. Amelia was 690 grams, tiny and perfect. But what horror to discover that William wasn't the 500 gram baby as they had been told to expect but a wee 320 grams! His liver was visible through his skin, you could see his heart beating; he was so tiny he looked like a 'special effects doll' for a movie. My son's wedding band fitted on his thigh. They said he wouldn't survive. Thankfully, he lived through the week-end. They decided he was a fighter so they too would join in his fight for life.

We asked many people to pray. There were people praying for the twins in England, USA, Germany, Papua New Guinea and in Africa. In fact, wherever any of us had friends and relatives, people prayed. And our little fighter grew and thrived. It was a miracle. Then came another disaster. A child was admitted to the ICU with a superbug. William caught it. He was on life support and wasn't expected to survive. There was more prayer the world over. And hooray … it was followed by another huge miracle.

Little William is now eight years old. He is very small for his age and has some challenges. However our miracle child is a feisty lively little person. The grief of Steve's death followed by the trauma of the twins' birth was a season I would never wish upon anyone.

But there were many blessings through it all. I discovered that I could lean on my church family and on my children and my siblings. I discovered that PRAYER was more powerful than medical opinion. I found that I could take anything to God my Father and that He would listen. I discovered that, when God's people pray together, amazing things happen.

I still miss my wonderful best friend, Steve. I miss our talks and the sharing of our lives and interests. But I do know that he is with his Lord and Saviour and that one day he and I will be re-united. Prayer was always a wonderful comfort, but since that time, my attitude to prayer has changed. In the past I prayed in hope. Now I pray in *expectation*.

God Spaces

My Stories – Seven

A small bush in our front garden had grown very quickly during the rainy season. It was a tiny bush when I'd last noticed it, but now it looked massive. A nearby bush had died some time before, leaving space for expansion. Have you noticed how plants often do that? They fill up the spaces in our gardens. Rainy seasons have a propensity of filling vacant spaces into places full of weeds.

I thought of the spaces in my life. There are often gaps that need filling. What do I fill up those spaces of my life with? Food? Entertainment? Shopping? TV? Facebook? Parties? Noise? Music? Other people? When a difficult season encroaches into my life—I have a few empty spaces waiting to be filled. There's nothing like hard times and rainy seasons to remind me of those spaces. And so, a wet season is a great time to discover those spaces which exist inside of me and to fill them with that which has eternal value.

A closer walk with God. Caring for others. Learning to love Jesus. Spending time with Him. Reading books that enhance my life. Building friendships that last. Using my gifts to bless the world around me. Becoming all I am created to be. How can I fill those spaces today? First, with God Himself, and next with eternal treasures.

Little Nuggets 8

Nuggets to help me through those stormy seasons

Words that bring Hope and Healing

Blessed is the one who trusts in the Lord, whose confidence is in Him.
Jeremiah 17:7 NIV

Guide me in your truth and teach me, for You are God my Saviour, and my hope is in You all day long.
Psalm 25:5 NIV

But the eyes of the Lord are on those who fear Him, on those whose hope is in His unfailing love.
Psalm 33:18 NIV

We wait in hope for the Lord; He is our help and our shield.
Psalm 33:20 NIV

May your unfailing love rest upon us, Lord, even as we put our hope in You.
Psalm 33:22 NIV

I must calm down and turn to God; He is my only hope.
Psalm 62:5 ERV

For You are my hope; O Lord God, You are my confidence from my youth.
Psalm 71:5 NASB

*How blessed is he whose help is the God of Jacob,
Whose hope is in the Lord his God.*

Psalm 146:5 NASB

*The Lord delights in those who fear Him, who
put their hope in His unfailing love.*

Psalm 147:11 NIV

*But as for me, I watch in hope for the Lord, I wait
for God my Saviour; my God will hear me.*

Micah 7:7 NIV

Hope

Poem 8

It looked dead,
its leaves
browned,
its branches withered,
the bush
in our garden.

A long dry summer had sapped its strength
and
as we gazed upon it
how sad we were
for not having
saved it.

It looked dead
but was it gone?

I started with surprise
when I saw the shoots
infinitesimal green shoots
starting out

*where deadness lived.
I could hardly believe it.
But yes,
tiny green
shoots
sprouted.*

*Perhaps …
it would live
after all.*

*That's what hope does
you know.*

*Brings
joy
where
sadness reigned,
ushers in
surprise
where
dismay dwelt.
Widens our eyes
in disbelief
but lights
a new lamp
of hope,
within.*

*What a faith we share
as believers,*

*fellow-heirs
in Christ,
knowing
with sure certainty
that Christ within
us
is our only hope
of glory.*

*A mystery
that's profound
but
simple,
a gem which is
true, rare,
and precious.*

*Hope!
It's yours.
Grab on to it
Today.*

*We
have a hope
that's indestructible,
sure
and steadfast.*

*A hope that began
at Calvary
and will*

*live on every day,
in every
circumstance.*

*Dispelling all despair
and lighting instead
the bright fire of joy
within.*

Sailing Paper Boats – Part 1

Turning lemons into lemonade.
Drawing close to God. A Hope Triumphant

Fill Thou my life, O Lord my God,
In every part with praise,
That my whole being may proclaim
Thy being and Thy ways.

Not for the lip of praise alone,
Nor e'en the praising heart
I ask, but for a life made up
Of praise in every part!

Praise in the common words I speak,
Life's common looks and tones,
In fellowship in hearth and board
With my beloved ones;

Fill every part of me with praise;
Let all my being speak
Of Thee and of Thy love, O Lord,
Poor though I be, and weak.

So shall each fear, each fret, each care

Be turned into a song,
And every winding of the way
The echo shall prolong;

So shall no part of day or night
From sacredness be free;
But all my life, in every step
Be fellowship with Thee.

Horatius Bonar

How do we turn every fear, every fret and every care into a song? How do we turn tragedy into triumph? Fear into hope? Despair into joy? Heartache into blessing? The short answer to that question is: '*Through Jesus*'.

Still, let me attempt the long answer. Have you sailed paper boats when you were a young child? I did and I had lots of fun in the doing of it. When the monsoon rains fell in Sri Lanka where I grew up, the drains filled up quickly. I remember my Dad helping us make paper boats. I can still feel the excitement bubbling inside of me as we dropped our little paper boats into the drain. To little eyes and little bodies that drain seemed to be a vast distance below the window.

I can picture those boats bobbing around in one drain and then … as we kids dashed to another window and peered out, we saw them turning up in the next drain. The soft white crumpled wet paper boats moved from drain to drain as the rain pattered down relentlessly.

What great fun … what sheer magic! And you know, we couldn't have sent them on their way unless the rains had fallen. Because the rain was needed to create a gushing 'river'. If it hadn't rained, we'd have missed the sight of those boats carried on their waters, like intoxicated sailors being flung along perilous seas.

When the rains of life pour down, we have the choice of sitting safe and sad inside our homes or running outdoors to send off a few paper boats in the choppy waters. Which would you rather do? I would prefer to safely remain indoors. But then, I'd miss out on all those moments of thrill and *adventure*. When I choose to sail paper boats in rainwater, I defy Satan's plans for me.

What then, are Satan's plans for me? Here are a few of them:

1. Feel sorry for myself
2. Be defeated
3. Give up
4. Stop trying
5. Blame God
6. Believe that life is dreadful
7. Have a pity party
8. Decide the paper boats will sink
9. Groan and moan
10. Infect the rest of the world with my negativity

Get the picture? Satan's plans diametrically oppose God's plans for us. Satan wants to make us fall down and stay down. He desires that we stop trusting God. He tries to make our misery ten times worse by tempting us to wallow in self-pity and turn our present season of difficulty into a permanent one.

During a stormy season in life, I told myself over and over again that I would make it. That, even if it didn't feel like it, it was only a temporary period and that God could make good come of it. That He could be trusted and that I could believe all of His promises. I didn't *feel* the truth of those statements. But my heart had already known the facts through years of experiencing God's faithfulness. So I forced myself to persevere in thinking positive thoughts and doing positive things.

And yes … after a while, it did bear good fruit. My tough season was actually a season of planting. Later, I came into a joyful season of reaping. *My rainwater had helped me sail paper boats in the storm.* As I recovered from the experience, God brought healing into my life. He turned my sadness into a song. He made rainbows out of rain. He changed me from the inside out.

So how do we do that in practical terms? Here are some of the lessons I learnt in making and sailing paper boats. I believe that the best thing that has happened because of my times of trouble is a greater closeness to Jesus. If not for those tough times … I would not have come to know Him as intimately, I would not have experienced His mighty power and strength, I would not have discovered His comfort, I would not have found in Him my Treasure.

Jesus shines bright in a storm—a lighthouse that sheds its beams across the dark, choppy seas. His bright rays of light will guide you safely to the shore—keeping you from sharks or jagged rocks, away from waves of destruction, secure from all those scary sea creatures—and He will lead you to a place of safety and Hope.

'Then they cried out to the Lord in their trouble, and He brought them out of their distress. He stilled the storm to a whisper; the waves of the sea were hushed. They were glad when it grew calm, and He guided them to their desired haven. Let them give thanks to the Lord for His unfailing love and His wonderful deeds for mankind. Let them exalt Him in the assembly of the people and praise Him in the council of the elders.' Psalm 107:28–32 NIV

Sailing Paper Boats – Part 2

Turning lemons into lemonade.
Drawing close to God. A Hope Triumphant

So what type of paper boat is best turned out of your soggy paper today? First, determine that you will use this season to get to know God better. Scripture tells us: *'Draw near to God and He will draw near to you.'* James 4:8 NIV

I have cried out to the Lord many times and have seen Him come through for me. I know He will do the same for you or perhaps He has done so already.

But how does one draw near to God? If you're not a Christian believer, there's something important to consider. Pray and ask God to open your eyes to your need of Him. Read the gospel of John and discover who Jesus is and what He accomplished for us. Jesus died for us. He took your sins and mine upon Himself. He defeated death and rose again. He promises eternal life to every person who places their trust in Him.

'For God so loved the world that He gave His one and only Son, that whoever believes in Him shall not perish but have eternal life.' John 3:16 NIV

'I assure you, anyone who hears what I say and believes in the One who sent Me has eternal life. They will not be judged guilty. They have already left death and have entered into life.' John 5:24 ERV

'Therefore, if anyone is in Christ, he is a new creation; old things have passed away; behold, all things have become new. Now all things are of God, who has

reconciled us to Himself through Jesus Christ, and has given us the ministry of reconciliation. 2 Corinthians 5:17–18 NKJV

As God warms your heart to know Him, open your heart to allowing Jesus to become the Lord and Saviour of your life. Jesus came to bring us peace with God through the forgiveness of our sins, so ask Him to forgive you for all sin. Commit your life to following Jesus and walking in His ways. His gift of new life is freely available to all who turn to Him. He responds to everyone who calls on His Name. Talk to a Christian if you want to understand more. Ask God to lead you into His ways for you. He will.

If you decide to make this commitment to Jesus (and I pray you do), it's the start of a glorious new relationship. And after that? You need to nurture it. The Bible says that becoming a follower of Jesus is like being '*born again*'. Spending time with Him on a regular basis is not just good to do, but essential. Reading the Bible, talking to God through prayer, spending time with other Christians are all-important. When I have been through difficult seasons, I have often come before Him with an open Bible and an open heart. I have asked Him to speak to me.

When I have gone to Him in tears, His comfort has been like a soft blanket around my shoulders. His presence blessed me and He healed my broken heart. There were times, though, when I was in too much pain to feel His presence. And if that is the place where you are at, that's ok too. Feelings are not the most important because they are liable to change. Facts are far more important. The truth is God promises that, as you draw near to Him in faith, He will draw near to you.

Have you ever written a *Gratitude Journal*? Write down everything you are thankful for. Praise God as you write it even if praise is difficult. Sometimes, you might feel there is little to thank Him for but, as you keep thanking Him, you will discover more reasons for thanksgiving.

There are times in my life when I've had a difficult person to contend with.

Writing a list of his or her positive qualities helped me focus on the good. It was tempting to dwell on one negative quality rather than on twenty positive ones. But having a list of those twenty positive qualities helped me fight the tendency to see only the bad.

'Rejoice always; pray continually; give thanks in all circumstances; for this is God's will for you in Christ Jesus.' 1 Thessalonians 5:16–18 NIV

Previously I said it was ok to grieve. And of the importance of laughter. Now I will add another layer to that truth. Aim also at being joyful. Grieve, but … be joyful. Hmmm … is that a contradiction in terms? Perhaps it is. But it's something I need to strive for, especially during those hard seasons. I need to choose joy. Joy is not a feeling. Joy is an *attitude*.

When life is difficult, our thoughts often go haywire. Prayer is a special gift God has blessed us with. Let's use it. Prayer has often delivered me and brought me healing and peace.

When troubling thoughts take hold of me, I've found a system of breaking negative patterns by using prayer.

1. I praise God for Jesus and all He has done for me.
2. I intercede for someone else who is in need of prayer.
3. I thank Him for a specific blessing in my life.

I keep using the formula (and other similar ones) each time I find my mind is fearful or negative. It forces me to focus on something positive and has helped break a negative thought cycle. It works.

Another type of paper boat is the link we can forge with others. Hard times often bring us closer to caring family and friends as nothing else does. Whenever I've leaned on my husband, my heart has leaped toward him in gratitude. We've become closer.

I remember a bewildering season when I lost my job, my ministry and my church family in one swoop. It was a painful time. However, my beloved was the dependable rock in my life that season, just as Jesus is the Rock I can stand on for all eternity. I thanked God for Shan then. I thank God for him now.

The truth is that there is a special gel that meshes people in need together. And so—the hard times turn into blessing—acquaintances may become close friends. Relationships are strengthened. And relationship is after all, what life is about.

'A snowflake is one of God's most fragile creations, but look what they can do when they stick together.' Unknown

So the best paper boats we can sail are …

1. 1. Drawing near to **God**
2. 2. Finding in Jesus our **Treasure**
3. 3. Practising a life of **Praise and Thanksgiving**
4. 4. Making **Prayer** our life breath
5. 5. Linking up with **Others**

'Before me, even as behind, God is, and all is well.'
John Greenleaf Whittier

May you rest today, secure in the arms of Him who loves you.

Every Monday – Part 8

A little story in ten parts

The next few days were even harder than usual. Sue dropped in for coffee one morning. She looked at my face, a question in her eyes. 'You seem more down than usual, Liz. Are you ok?'

I opened my mouth to tell her about the note but the words were stuck in my throat. I knew I was being unreasonable. I knew I was being silly. But there it was. I felt that the closeness I had felt to Peter every Monday was coming to an end. *How would I bear it?*

The night before the 17th, I had a nightmare. I dreamt I was standing in a never-ending line at a shopping centre. A clown came by and waved a flag near my face. The flag had the words: '*No more Mondays! No more Mondays!*' written across it in large zig-zag black letters. I flinched and screamed. I woke up, sweating. I sat up in bed and cried. I cried for Peter. I cried for what might have been. I cried because I missed him so.

It was 9 a.m. on that final Monday. I was washing up my breakfast cereal bowl, when the doorbell rang. I stopped. My heart thumped a little harder than usual. I breathed in slowly. 'Calm down, Liz,' I told myself. *'Calm down.'*

I went to open the door. Perhaps it would be one of the children dropping by. I knew they'd all drop in some time—that day being the first anniversary of their dad's death.

I hesitated for a couple of seconds. Then I walked quickly to the door. I opened it. I noticed that the sky was an unusual colour—a mixture of blue and grey. A lone thrush sat on a branch of the gum tree in my front yard. He was singing his heart out. Pretty pink geraniums were growing in profusion, now that spring had arrived. In spite of myself, I drank in the loveliness and almost enjoyed the sight. I looked down upon the welcome mat. It was there. Not a gift this time. But a letter. And no piece of paper next to it, this time.

Yes, it *was* the last one.

...to be continued

Michelle's Story

Friends' Stories 8

'I say to myself, "The Lord is my portion; therefore I will wait for Him."'
Lamentations 3:24 NIV

Trying to comfort and help a friend is always satisfying? Right. Wrong. Well … not always. It usually does, but there are exceptions—it sometimes messes with your own deep well of joy. That's what happened to me. I'd been ministering to a friend who was struggling with trust issues. As I listened to her across many conversations, she became brighter and thanked me for comforting her. Of course, it was exactly what I wanted to hear. But then … I would walk away feeling downhearted. I was weighed down, like I was carrying a huge boulder on my back. I was taking her issues back home with me. It meant that her sadness and her situation affected everything I did.

Then came the 'eureka' moment. I recognised where it all came from.

I realised that the defeated one had no new tricks to bring my way and catch me off-guard. He uses the same old tricks because he knows my weaknesses. No matter how much I had forgiven others, the past had a way of creeping up in unexpected ways. As many difficult memories kept returning to haunt me, I started re-living the difficult times my family had been through. It was far from pleasant.

What could I do? How could I break out of it? Even as I was deeply aware of my weakness … the Lord brought to my mind a verse from the book of Romans. I realised with great joy I could renew my mind afresh.

'Do not conform to the pattern of this world, but be transformed by the renewing of your mind. Then you will be able to test and approve what God's will is—His good, pleasing and perfect will.' Romans 12:2 NIV

That was it—that was what I had to do. I knew then that renewing my mind was not something I should do just occasionally. I needed to renew my mind *every single day.*

I opened my heart and mind to God again, this time on a daily basis. Was God faithful? *Of course He was.* I was able to minister to my friend, then walk away without carrying her burdens or being struck down by painful memories. I was free at last. Praise God that it's possible to renew my mind every day through the power of His Holy Spirit.

In front of the Mirror

My Stories – Eight

It was a blustery, wet winter's day and I was getting ready for my evening walk. I'd borrowed my son's blue raincoat and tried to button it on the go. It had navy blue studs at the top and Velcro all the way down. As I kept walking, I'd tried hard to make the studs work, but I couldn't see them. So I tried to connect the velcro sections, but that too turned out to be a big challenge.

A few days later, I donned my son's raincoat a second time and decided to button it up *before* I left home. Standing in front of the mirror, I could easily see the studs. It was no problem to put them together. I was surprised the top of the jacket fit snugly. The other day, I'd assumed that the studs were missing. The velcro was super simple too as, with the mirror's expert guidance, I could see where each part fit.

What a pleasant surprise to find my son's lovely blue raincoat fitted me after all. I had assumed it was a bad fit because my son was taller. I had found it bulky simply because I hadn't buttoned it up correctly. I marvelled to myself at the difference the mirror had made. A rainy day. A walk in the rain. A raincoat that worked perfectly. How did that work out? Because I had looked at what I was doing.

'Do not merely listen to the Word, and so deceive yourselves. Do what it says. Anyone who listens to the Word but does not do what it says is like someone who looks at his face in a mirror and, after looking at himself, goes away and

immediately forgets what he looks like. But whoever looks intently into the perfect law that gives freedom, and continues in it—not forgetting what they have heard, but doing it—they will be blessed in what they do.' James 1:22–25 NIV

We look into a mirror in order to correct ourselves. We look into the Bible for guidance and direction—to find out what is wrong in us and to correct it. If I notice a smudge on my face, wouldn't it be silly if I walked away without wiping it off? The Bible teaches me among other things how to 'dress in rainy weather'. When I am going through a tough season of my life, I can dress appropriately for it by reading the Word, studying it and finding the best way to dress my mind with the right attitude.

When the rainy seasons arrived, I have found through the Word, a wonderful peace and a beautiful covering for my mind in the midst of the storms.

As I walked in the rain that day in a snugly fitted raincoat, I stayed cosy and dry and enjoyed my evening walk. I was finally dressed right. And now, through this rainy season too, I dress with His *Word* in my mind, His *Promises* deep inside my heart and His *Hope* burning brightly within.

Little Nuggets 9

Nuggets to help me through those stormy seasons

Praise lifts me above my circumstances and brings me to a place of freedom from negative thoughts and unhelpful patterns. Praise God because He is worthy. Praise Him when you can. Praise Him even when you find it hard due to difficult circumstances. It may be the best present you give both God and yourself. Try it.

MY PRAISE LIST: I praise YOU, Lord, for ...

1. Jesus
2. My faith
3. The gift of music
4. Your amazing love
5. Your Word
6. Your kindness
7. Your generosity
8. Your provision
9. Having nothing to fear
10. Mercies that are new every day
11. Your faithfulness
12. Creation
13. Accepting me
14. The gift of prayer
15. The Cross
16. Daily blessings
17. Forgiveness
18. Freedom
19. My church family
20. Your goodness
21. Changing me
22. Your Holy Spirit
23. Being Unchanging
24. Being the King of kings
25. Being the Lord of lords
26. Reigning over the earth
27. Your sovereignty
28. Being God with us
29. Your wisdom
30. Being Omnipresent
31. Your Mercy
32. Your Grace

Season of Growth

Poem 9

Lord,
It is hard for me,
So hard for me
To wait,
To stay,
To be still
This moment.

But Lord,
I want to thank you for
Your Schoolroom
where
patience is taught
Others (and not self) are brought into focus
Relationships take on new meaning
And where love is the key.

Yes, Lord,
I need to say thank you
For hard lessons
Well taught.

*For difficult days
which deepen into soul growth
For the times
when
I would rather
Do what I want
Not what you ask of me.
But your love
Drives me on
To become the
person
I am meant to be.*

*Oh Father
You ask me today
to be still
To refrain
From effort
And instead
To stay by You.*

*And so
I will be still
And know
That you are God.*

*I will be still.
I will be aware
of the
wonder
of*

Your Love.

*Thank you Lord
For this season of
growth!*

*I will
Be still.*

How Green is my Valley – Part 1

Rain brings life and growth; Hope fulfilled

During our South Australian summers, we usually have little rain. And so, after the glory of springtime, summers often bring scorching temperatures, a parched cracked earth, brown grass—a world that lacks the vibrant, refreshing colours of earlier months.

What a difference a little rain made! As I drove around our neighbourhood, I was amazed how fresh and green the world looked. Later, when I took a ride on our Adelaide O-bahn—a special bus on rails—I enjoyed seeing lush grass-carpets, gurgling brooks and breathtaking scenery. Yes, the rain had brought both colour and growth. It had fulfilled my hopes for an enchanting world.

When we encounter rainy seasons, we may baulk at the way the world treats us. But, just as nature needs the rain in order to create green pastures, we too cannot enjoy growth and 'greenness of soul' unless some rain falls into our lives.

'Storms make oaks take deeper roots.'

George Herbert

It's true. No storms in life? No roots. Oh well—perhaps some shallow roots but not deep ones. I can say without a shadow of doubt I'd be a far more selfish, self-absorbed person if I hadn't encountered the storms of life. I would have also been pretty superficial. I would not have been able to empathise as much. I would not have liked myself as much as I do now. I would have short, stumpy roots. Yes, I am sure I've grown in leaps and bounds through my tough seasons. *No doubt about that.*

What kinds of growth can we look forward to as we persevere through rainy seasons? What kind of blessing? We often grow closer to God when we seek Him during our storms. We also grow in relationship, in our connection with others and in our relationship with ourselves.

The older I grow, the more important relationships have become. My gifts and abilities, achievements and moments of glory, my acquisitions and earthly treasures all come second to relationship. None of these bring anything near the kind of joy and richness my connection with family and friends have given me. I'm so grateful to God for my husband, my son, my parents, my brothers and sisters, my church family, our extended family, friends, even my acquaintances—all who have added depth to my life. My life would not be as fulfilled without their presence, their love and what they have taught me.

A big help in recovering from our tough times is *blessing others*. Sometimes it's too hard to do. When we are in deep pain—it's not easy to reach out and to bless another. It's enough to just struggle on living. And yet, it is often the very medicine we need and could pour soothing oil over our hurting, inflamed wounds.

Is there someone else who's in need? Perhaps you could reach out and let them know you care. Perhaps you could use your own pain to empathise with them. Perhaps you could comfort others with the comfort that you received from God? Yes, helping others in need benefits those you help and also blesses you.

I remember a time when life had been difficult. As I went to my volunteer job at my church office, I asked God to use my sadness for good. Did He? Oh yes. He brought into our office a lady who'd been to prison. My heart grieved with her over what she had been through. She was not a bad person, but life had been hard for her and she'd shoplifted to feed her children.

With tears in my eyes I listened. I heard her. My own pain made me more sensitive to hers. True, I hadn't encountered what she had been through. But I too had been through pain of a different kind which helped me empathise and care. I offered to pray with her. At once, she said, 'Yes'. It was a very special moment. I knew God was with us. I could sense His presence as I prayed.

One year later, she came back. This time, I was led to share the gospel with her and she came to know Jesus. She told me then, that the year before—when I'd had first prayed with her—it had been the first time she'd realised there was really a God above who cared for her. She'd started talking to God after we prayed together and she'd continued to talk to Him ever since.

Let's re-consider a verse I quoted at the beginning of this book. But this time, let's look at some verses following it. *'Praise be to the God and Father of our Lord Jesus Christ, the Father of compassion and the God of all comfort, who comforts us in all our troubles, so that we can comfort those in any trouble with the comfort we ourselves have received from God.'*

For just as we share abundantly in the sufferings of Christ , so also our comfort abounds through Christ. If we are distressed, it is for your comfort and salvation; if we are comforted, it is for your comfort, which produces in you patient endurance of the same sufferings we suffer. And our hope for you is firm, because we know that just as you share in our sufferings, so also you share in our comfort.'
2 Corinthians 1:3–7 NIV

How Green is my Valley – Part 2

Rain brings life and growth; Hope fulfilled

Over the years, many family and friends have helped me when I was in distress. *How they have blessed me!* I'm very fortunate to have a husband who's an excellent listener. These past twelve years as I've struggled with chronic illness, it could not have been easy for him hearing his wife's constant moans and groans over her battle with the relentless fibromyalgia. Oh, but he's blessed me time and time again with his understanding and empathy. I always feel much lighter when I 'unload' my troubles into his listening ears because it makes all the difference to my pain. *How blessed I am!*

When God (sometimes through others) comforts us in our times of grief—we have a unique set of tools to help us care for others—we have empathy and sensitivity, sharpened by our own suffering and pain. On occasion I've had tears well up in my own eyes as I've listened to someone in pain. I have been embarrassed at my emotional reaction to their pain, but then … it comforted the person I was ministering to in a way that nothing else would.

During my season of grief and pruning which I've mentioned before, God showed me what my heart was like. There was pride, selfishness, thoughtlessness, lack of discipline, rebellion against God and desire for the approval of others over His approval. With deep shock and sadness, I saw the magnitude of my own sin—an affront to a Holy God. I realised then that I could always empathise with others who sin or who go through difficult times. We are all of us in the same place—sinful frail creatures in need of His grace. God taught me then to look at others with a heart of grace, just as His grace covers me.

Though tough times brought me closer to others, there are times when God pulled the rug from under my feet and has made me rely on Him alone. That's been good too. He has strong shoulders, others don't. In the first place, it's not fair to place that kind of burden on others by leaning too much on them. Only God has His *God hat* on. I sure can't take His place, so I'll not even try.

So while it is true that our relationships deepen as we go through tough times, it's also true that we need to have God at the centre of our lives. It will ensure that all other relationships will be healthy and beneficial. Our tough times will help us to be more loving, empathetic, less judgmental and more giving.

Have you heard of the story of the egg and the potato? When the egg is dropped in boiling water, it becomes hard. When the potato is popped into that same boiling water, it becomes soft. *Which do I aspire to be? Hard or soft?*

There are two opposing ways of responding to tough times. Viktor Frankl spent four years in a concentration camp. He lost his parents and his wife. The only family member left was his sister, but the amazing truth was that he didn't emerge bitter through his experiences. Instead, he offered meaning and richness to the world through all he had encountered. In his book, *Man's Search for Meaning*, Frankl observes there is one thing that no one can take away from us. That is *attitude*.

And so ... I realise it's not what happens to me that's the prime director of my happiness. It's my *response* to life that matters. I can be embittered and cynical through life's storms, or I can grow through it all. I am never a victim. Through Christ, I am always a victor.

What are the lessons to be learned through the stormy seasons?

1. **Is God testing my faith**? *If He is, has my faith grown stronger?*

2. **Is He correcting me?** *What do I need to change in my life? My actions or words, thoughts or attitudes?*

3. **Is He humbling me** because I have been too full of myself or have I been proud? *Have I learnt to be humble?*

4. **Is He protecting me** from something worse? *Have I thanked Him for His protection?*

5. **Should I change my own direction**? *Where am I headed? Should I stop and move in a new direction?*

'God whispers to us in our pleasures, speaks to us in our conscience, but shouts in our pains: it is His megaphone to rouse a deaf world.' C.S. Lewis

God has certainly roused a deaf *Anusha* through His megaphone called pain. After I've ignored His clear messages to me, God has finally got through to me through pain.

Here are some of the truths He taught me through my tough seasons:

1. The meaning of the *Cross* and why He came to earth

2. The magnitude of my *sin* before Him, a Holy God

3. The magnitude of His amazing *Grace* toward me

4. Why I need *Jesus* so

5. To *empathise* with others no matter what their situation

6. *Humility*—it's vital in the Kingdom life

7. To *listen* to Jesus

8. To learn to give Him *my all* every day for the rest of my life
9. To let *Him increase* and to allow myself to decrease
10. To be *pure, holy and blameless* through His Holy Spirit
11. To *forgive* others just as He forgave me
12. The *responsibility* of being the right *witness* through my *life* and through my *writing*

As I look back on all I've encountered I am deeply blessed. The seasons of grief and pain have given away to seasons of growth, change and blessing. I would not exchange much of what I've been through. Even though the rainy seasons seemed too difficult to manoeuvre through at the time—they did come to an end. They brought me a season of singing. My soul experienced growth and I have been filled.

How green is my valley!

Every Monday – Part 9

A little story in ten parts

I picked up the letter, looked around for a moment. A wild wind stirred, scattering some fallen leaves. The thrush flew away. All at once, a patch of sunlight shone brightly through the leaves of the gum tree and dazzled my eyes. I went in and shut the door. I sat down, tore open the envelope and took the letter out with trembling fingers.

It was in my husband's handwriting. *He had written it!* When? How? How did it get here?

> *Darling sweet Lizzie,*
>
> *When you read this I will be no more. But I had to write it. Because you see, I want you to know that no matter what happens, I will always be close to you. Every day, every hour. The cancer that robbed my life didn't take away our 33 years together. You will still have memories. You will still have my love. I may not be around in my body, but our love will last forever.*
>
> *So, darling Lizzie, don't be sad. I know you will grieve, but don't grieve too long. Life has not ended for you yet! You know it hasn't, even though you may feel it has. I hope you enjoyed the little gifts I arranged for you. I had such fun planning them—you know me, don't you? I asked Simon to do the deliveries. (Simon was Peter's*

best mate) I knew I could count on him. Did you enjoy them? They came with the biggest batch of love from my heart.

Thank you for all you have been to me as my wife and life's partner. You have meant so much to me over the years, especially during the last 2 months when life was very difficult. I could not have gotten through that time without you. Thank you Lizzie, my darling; my wife; my best friend!

I want you to remember the good times we shared together. And then, you know of course, darling Lizzie, that for those of us who know Jesus—death is not the end. It is the beginning to a brand new life. You and I will spend eternity together. So cling onto that thought and live fully after I am gone. I will be cheering you on.

And don't forget….I will always love you.

Forever Yours,

Pete

…to be continued

Sylvia's Story

Friends' Stories 9

I was looking forward to an exciting and fulfilling year. I was working in a job with an excellent salary, transport to and from work, unlimited medical entitlement and a yearly bonus of four months' pay. Everything went smoothly and enjoyably at first. Suddenly things at my workplace began to change. I found I was very often the butt of unkind remarks by senior colleagues.

In spite of the unpleasant atmosphere, I stuck with my job. My husband encouraged me to keep going. He thought I was being unnecessarily affected by the jibes which, he guessed, stemmed from envy. He would often give me positive maxims to read. *'The higher you climb in life, there will be many people wanting to pull you down. Do not be affected but continue unfailingly until you reach the heights.'*

That year my beloved dad passed away. I loved my father very much and I grieved deeply when he died. He would always give the benefit of the doubt to people who arrived at our home with hard luck stories. A favourite saying of his was: *'There but for the grace of God go I.'* I saw in him many characteristics of Christ.

Concentrating on my work was difficult. I would suddenly burst into tears. There was no one to comfort me. I felt alone. Three months later I had an operation to remove a nodule on my thyroid gland. After recuperating at home for two weeks, I returned to my workplace, glad that I had survived the operation.

But soon, I was reprimanded for something I didn't do. It was a story made up by a senior colleague. My attempts at proving it was not true fell on deaf ears. It was too much for me. I felt vulnerable, helpless, friendless. Bursting into tears, I said I would tender my resignation. Office policy required that six months' notice had to be given when resigning, so I gave in my letter on at the beginning of June. I continued going to work, knowing that in December I would be free.

That year turned out to be the one my decision to follow Christ some time previously would be officially confirmed in my church. Confirmation classes were held on Saturdays. I combined my visits to my parents' home with these classes. We studied the story of Joseph which inspired me greatly. I became more interested in my work. I eventually left my workplace, not having obtained another permanent job. However the encouragement of family members helped me to find temporary employment.

The following year was a very tough time for me. Life has had its usual share of ups and downs since then, but God has spoken to me, encouraged me and guided me many times through others: family members, uncles, aunts, cousins and friends. When I look back at that year that seemed like the end of the world, I believe all these experiences were necessary in order to build me up.

In the midst of it all, I had a life-changing experience. While sitting on my bed reading the Bible, I felt a slight breeze come through the open window and gently move the curtains.

The next moment I felt the Presence of Someone standing at the foot of the bed. I was enveloped with a sense of warmth and security. I knew then what it must be like to be in my mother's womb. Secure. Safe. Comforted. I was enfolded in so deep a love my whole being yearned for that moment to last forever. It must have happened in the blink of an eye. As soon as I tried to reason it out, the Presence left. I know it was God Himself coming to comfort and sustain me.

What assurance it brought me. He confirmed me in His love and His presence and His comfort. I am so thankful that He is in my life and has always brought me through.

Unseen

My Stories – Nine

As I wended my way around the Oval that night, I was thrilled to see a silvery moon beaming down from behind a clump of hazy soft cotton clouds. It lit my path with a bright pool of light. As I began my third lap of the Oval, I looked up. The white clouds had dispersed, leaving in their wake a vast bank of murky grey clouds. What of the moon? It wasn't visible anymore. Those grey clouds seemed to have swallowed it up.

What a good illustration of God's reality in our times of need. Too often we imagine He hasn't heard us—or has moved away. But of course He hasn't. He is near, far closer than we realise. He's by us with ears open towards us and a heart filled with love. Circumstance might veil His tender face from our gaze, like those murky clouds hid the moon that night. Just because I don't see Him doesn't mean He isn't near me. Just because I don't feel Him doesn't mean He is withholding His love from me.

He is present. He is closer than my breath.

And nothing can ever separate me from His love.

Little Nuggets 10

Nuggets to help me through those stormy seasons

Wisdom for Tough Times

1. Fix my eyes on Jesus—not on my circumstances—Hebrews 12:1.

2. Let God use my suffering to refine my spirit.

3. Seek to develop the fruit of the Spirit through my hard times: *Love, joy, peace, patience, kindness, goodness, faithfulness, gentleness, self-control.*

4. Being crushed is very difficult. Allow the fragrance of my suffering touch others.

5. The centre of His will is the safest place for me. Stay there.

6. Don't lean on just one, two or three people all the time. Some friends will walk part of my journey, others the next. Don't make one person my only refuge—it's not only too big a burden but it gives them the place that belongs to God. Of course my spouse or best friend can be a sure help and, if so, that's wonderful. But it's wise to look to many sources of help.

7. Remember as I suffer that God's love is present and will never change.

8. A new beginning will arrive one day. I will wait for it.

9. God forgives. Always. So if I've messed up, it's ok.

10. With God's help, I will use my season of grief to bless others.

11. It's easy to misunderstand others when I am hurting. I will try to let go of my expectations. I will forgive those who don't understand, those who judge me and those who refuse to help me.

12. *Being* is more important than *doing*. And that's what trials often do—they change me from the inside out. Let God change me. The fruit of such change will be sweet.

13. Storms don't last forever. The sun will shine again.

14. God is my refuge and strength. He is a Very Present Help in trouble.

15. I shall be drenched in grace. His grace is *always* available.

16. With God's help, I will relish the *good* days—I will keep track of them. I will write about my happy times. I will read them to help me when I feel blue.

17. With God's help, I will choose my attitude—I will choose JOY—
1 Thessalonians 5:16–18

18. With God's help, I will not compare my journey with others.

19. Letting go is always important. With God's help, I will try my best to *let go.*

20. With God's help, I will see the big picture.

21. With God's help, I will ask others to pray for me when I need their support.

22. With God's help, I will tell myself often that I will feel better soon. *I will.*

23. With God's help, I will imagine what life will be like when the sun shines again and I shall anticipate it with glad expectation.

24. Life is sometimes full of pain but life is good.

25. God is good. Always. Every moment. He will fulfill His purposes in my life.

Jan's Story

Friends' Stories 10

The Heart of God

*The heart of God is stronger
Than the heart of man can know
Because it doesn't bear the sin
That the heart of man will show.
When the heart of man is full of pain
His soul despairing and low
The heart of God is grieving
And feels with us, blow by blow.*

*We tell Him we will not regain
Our spirit's former glow
Because this aching heart of man
Can only feel pure woe.*

*But when we're done with weeping
And our tears have ceased to flow
The heart of God can comfort
Where the heart of man can't go.*

The heart of God will move right in

And seeds of strength re-sow,
And gently, firmly, bring us back
Where we mightn't want to go.

Then the heart of man can recognise
The heart of God overflow
with love, and respond with confidence
and receive a joy unknown.

And the heart of God can be trusted
To slowly ease the pain
and return to us the faith we'd thought
we'd never know again.

Because the heart of God's more loving
than the heart of man can know
until we need its fullness
And in agony we go.

To the garden where our Brother
Poured out His grief and pain
And wished that to the Father He could go once again
Without the need to die cruel death and take on all our blame.
And when we feel His pain we
See the heart of God again
And know that we can but accept
the heart of God made plain.

The Darkest hour is before the Dawn

Poem 10

*We live
in a crazy old
upside down
world.*

*A world
which knows
discord
and disarray;
a world
where
darkness
reigns,
where distress
is rampant.*

*It is
a world that's
torn apart
by sin,
suffering,*

strife.

*A world
that has lost its way somewhere
as it journeys around the
sun.*

*But....
the light
of the glory
of the gospel
shines
in the night,
And in the darkest of
places.*

*One beautiful day,
good
will triumph
over evil,
justice
will prevail over
every injustice,
right
will rule
over all the wrongs
the world
has ever known.*

*Thank God for Jesus
whose*

*bright
light
dispels
the shadows,
whose joy
illumines
the bleakest
corner,
whose
radiance
is a soft but brilliant
beacon
in a world
that
has forgotten
its Creator.*

*Thank God
for Jesus;*

*He is the
Light of
our world!*

*He shines brightest
when the night has
reached its
darkest hour.*

*Thank God
for*

Jesus!

*One day the world will
find its light
As it travels
around the Son.*

*His light
will
never be
extinguished.*

*His brightness will
illuminate the world;
not just today,
but also
tomorrow,
next year,
a hundred years from now
&
throughout
all eternity.*

*Thank God
for Jesus.*

*He is
the Light
of the World!*

And Best of All – Part 1

And best of all… God is with us.

After serving for seven years as a university lecturer, my husband Shan was about to take a well-earned sabbatical. Life in Sri Lanka at the time was uncertain. A war raged. Some days, I'd have to rush to retrieve our five-year-old before school closed because of recurrent bomb threats. It was a difficult time.

Shan and I prayed God would lead us into the best future for us. His sabbatical opening up in Malaysia seemed to be the way forward. We didn't know then that God would lead us to migrate to Australia. But that day, God spoke to me very distinctly through a Scriptural verse. '*The Lord Himself goes before you and will be with you. He will never leave you nor forsake you. Do not be afraid; do not be discouraged.*' Deuteronomy 31:8 NIV

I'd seen this verse just a few days before. Now, it kept turning up, all over the place—inside a greeting card, as I studied the Word, in a few other spots—the details are fuzzy now. But every time I read the verse, it resonated deep within, a message given *just for me*. It was like an email that landed in the inbox of my heart straight from my Papa God.

Its meaning was clear. First, as we left Sri Lanka's shores for foreign lands, God promised to go before us. (Thank You, Lord!) Next, He seemed to declare life would bring many difficult seasons. (Oh dear! *Not* what I wanted to hear.) But finally and most importantly, God told me clearly through the verse that *we need never be afraid because He would always be with us and would never ever leave us.*

Five times He spoke to me and five times I heard Him. I took it seriously. The promise was like a long drink of cold water on a hot day—a deep deep knowledge that God was not only in control of our future but would always be with us. The three of us stepped aboard a plane that took us far away from all things familiar and people we loved. I decided to believe His promise for us. That was twenty years ago.

The subsequent two decades have brought both pleasure and pain, blessed moments and difficult ones. Seasons of sunshine and seasons of rain. Seasons of sowing and seasons of reaping. Sometimes there was little sunshine as rainclouds threatened. Sometimes we were immersed in a deluge that went on and on. But one thing that has stood out for me during those years, like the bright glow of the evening star, is the faithfulness of a loving God.

Just as He promised, God was with us and He brought us through. I remember one particularly difficult day. I was distraught, in pain, in tears. I'd written to a friend asking her to pray for me. I didn't give her any details; only mentioned that I needed prayer. She wrote back at once. She sent me the verse, Deuteronomy 31:8 NIV, '*The Lord Himself goes before you and will be with you. He will never leave you nor forsake you. Do not be afraid. Do not be discouraged.*'

I was stunned! She didn't know the importance of what I'd come to call my *life verse*. But she'd listened to God, and He comforted me through her. What a blessed assurance! God knew my pain. He was with me through my time of trial. He would bring me safely through.

As we contemplate the rainy seasons in our lives and the slush they bring, we also catch a glimpse of their enrichment in our lives. God is alive and active in the world today. He came to earth in the person of Jesus Christ to bring freedom and forgiveness of sins, light and hope to each of us. He is my Treasure. He is totally dependable. He is Almighty. He is present everywhere, anywhere, all of the time. He is holy. He is love.

The rainy seasons have also brought me a deeper understanding of others. These seasons have helped me bond closer with others. Relationships have deepened. Understanding has flourished. How selfish I would be if not for life's storms.

The rainy seasons have also brought me a deeper understanding of myself. They have helped me grow in character. Character growth isn't enjoyable while it's happening. Watch a stubborn toddler trying to make a statement to his mum. His will is exercised. His lungs are powerful. His voice is loud. His face is red. His tantrum cannot be ignored. No two-year-old likes character growth.

No sixty-year-old likes character growth either.

I wonder where you are today in life's journey. Are you in a place of deep grief? I grieve with you, dear friend. Are you hanging in there, praying for the storm to pass? It's a good decision. Keep on keeping on. I do know your storm will pass. Afterwards it will usher in life and growth, fulfilment and peace. You have not just my word for it, but God's Word and God's Word is always reliable.

'You see, at just the right time, when we were still powerless, Christ died for the ungodly. Very rarely will anyone die for a righteous person, though for a good person someone might possibly dare to die. But God demonstrates his own love for us in this: While we were still sinners, Christ died for us.' Romans 5:8 NIV

If He died while we were broken—doesn't it mean then that He decided we were worth dying for? That there was hope for us after all? That all of us broken people were worth fixing?

2 Corinthians 4:7–10 NIV gives us something to hold onto: *'But we have this treasure in jars of clay to show that this all-surpassing power is from God*

and not from us. We are hard-pressed on every side, but not crushed; perplexed, but not in despair; persecuted, but not abandoned; struck down, but not destroyed. We always carry around in our body the death of Jesus, so that the life of Jesus may also be revealed in our body.'

There's the secret of learning to live through the hard times. As St Paul expressed so well—we are hard-pressed but not crushed. We are often perplexed, but we do not need to give into despair. We are conquerors through Him who loved us.

Every Monday – Part 10

A little story in ten parts

I read the letter through. My eyes misted over and the tears fell again. But this time, my mouth curved upwards into a smile. There was wonder, surprise, and even a tinge of joy in my heart. It *was* Peter who reached me through these gifts. It *was* he who had planned them all. *I should have known!*

As I cried, I remembered the good times I had enjoyed with him. It was then I knew that my healing had begun. No more Mondays. But then, I didn't need Mondays any more. This letter from Peter, reaching me a year after he died was the best gift I had received. To think he had planned it all during those painful months of his illness touched me no end. It was just like him. Not thinking of his own pain during those difficult months but of me and how *I* would cope.

I would read the letter every day and feel his love. No—his love for me had not died, nor mine for him. Love lives on forever! I knew that now. His memory would remain fresh and vibrant in my heart—always. And one glad day I would dance on the streets of heaven with him.

I got up and put the kettle on.

It was time to live again!

And Best of All – Part 2

And best of all… God is with us.

If Jesus hadn't come into the world, our suffering would be simply be that. Suffering! But the arrival of Jesus turned it 180 degrees. Suffering has a purpose, so suffering is considered a privilege for those of us who know Him. Let's reflect again on a verse I shared at the beginning of this book.

'For it has been granted to you on behalf of Christ not only to believe on Him, but also to suffer for Him.' Philippians 1:29 NIV

The good news is that through Jesus, suffering has meaning. If suffering has meaning, perhaps it is not a bad thing after all. Perhaps it's something we can embrace?

Viktor Frankl points out in *Man's Search for Meaning*: *'Our patients never really despair because of any suffering in itself. Instead, their despair stems in each instance from a doubt as to whether suffering is meaningful. Man is ready and willing to shoulder any suffering as soon and as long as he can see a meaning in it.'*

St Paul spoke words of life and victory to the Corinthian church: *'Therefore we do not lose heart. Though outwardly we are wasting away, yet inwardly we are being renewed day by day. For our light and momentary troubles are achieving for us an eternal glory that far outweighs them all. So we fix our eyes not on what is seen, but on what is unseen. For what is seen is temporary, but what is unseen is eternal.'* 2 Corinthians 4:16–18 NIV

In every good narrative, the classic *'things are not what they seem'* plot helps us keep turning the pages. A twist at the end of the story often makes a heart-stopping finish. In God's story too, things are not what they seem.

Are you suffering physically with pain that is hard to bear? Are you struggling financially? Is your heart broken after a relationship that went wrong? Have you been accused of wrongdoing when you have been a person of integrity? Is there no one who understands what you are going through? Do you have estranged family relationships causing you deep distress? Are you grieving the loss of a loved one? Have you been abused or mistreated? Has life been a series of difficult seasons playing over and over again? Do you feel alone or discarded?

Take heart, my friend. *Things are not what they seem.* Jesus has overcome. Life right now might look like a picture destroyed by big blobs of black paint thrown over the bright colours, spoiling their beauty. The truth is that what you are experiencing is not the final picture. There is more. Although outwardly you may be wasting away every day, inwardly you are being renewed like the eagle. The reason Scripture calls our troubles both light and momentary is because, in the balance of eternity, that is what they are. Our lives on earth span 70, 80, 90 years … give or take. In comparison with eternity, these years are but a moment. Our burdens cannot be compared to the joys of heaven awaiting us.

When a hurricane tears into my life, sudden and unexpected, I can cling onto the hope I have in Jesus. He is working on my behalf even when I don't see it. In the world's economy, suffering implies weakness or defeat. But Satan's ploy of crucifying our Saviour fell flat. The laugh is on our enemy. He thought he had defeated God but we know very differently. It was the biggest victory possible. Jesus' death and resurrection freed all of Creation from sin's grasp. Death and sin were wallowed up in victory. Death lost its sting and its power was forever broken.

When we suffer according to God's will—we reach a place of hope and promise and our suffering becomes precious and valuable. Genesis 1:1 says: *'In the beginning, God…'*. He was. He is. He is the Great I Am. I like stories with happy endings, don't you? The Bible tells us that God's story has a resounding finish.

Do you believe it?

This insight gives me hope when I take a tumble and I am caught gasping for breath. It keeps me going when I feel like giving up. It helps me get up again when I fall into a rainy day mud puddle. It keeps me *Dancing in the Rain*.

Who's the number one person in the life today? Your spouse? Your son or daughter? Your Mum or Dad? Your best friend? An actor or actress? A cricketer or football player? A comedian? Your dog or your cat? We all have people we hold near and dear to our hearts. Having them near brings you life and hope and joy. Losing them would mean the end of the world as we know it.

The problem though is that even those closest to us disappoint us. We are born sinful. We are all far from perfect. Friends might betray my trust or mistreat me. And of course even the most wonderful person will die one day and I cannot hold onto him forever. There's only One Person who can ride out any and every storm with us. Jesus. He will *never* let you down. If bad times happen—He will use it to enhance your story. If He the God of the Universe is on your side, what have you to fear?

'If God is for us, who can be against us? He who did not spare His own Son, but gave Him up for us all—how will He not also, along with Him, graciously give us all things?" Romans 8:31–32 NIV

I do believe though that when we are yielded to His will and do our best to live His way through the help of His Holy Spirit—God will bring beauty out of ashes and the oil of joy through mourning. He might return to you what was lost, or He will give it back to you in a different way altogether. He does give us all things—the 'all things' we need. Life. Wholeness. Eternal Life. Love. The Fruit of the Holy Spirit. He gives to us from the abundant stores of His grace. Forgiveness. Beauty. Goodness. Truth. A Glorious Ending that's beyond death. LIFE after life.

So if you have lost a loved one through death—cling on to the hope you have in Jesus. We in Christ know that death is not the end for those who walk with God. Jesus has conquered both life and death. One day, you will be re-united with your loved one.

As I sat refining this book, I placed the following status on Facebook: *Anusha Atukorala is chopping, changing, cutting, pasting, slashing, refining, and wielding her editor's brain over my current manuscript. 'Twill be rather a battered manuscript by the end of the day, poor thing. But hopefully will turn out better for it :)*

My work-in-progress was definitely having a hard time of it. Some of the chapters didn't know themselves as I moved them around. But without that refining process, it would not have been as good. And that's exactly what God does in our lives. Without the storms, I would always remain a first draft. Not a publishable copy. Not one worth sharing with the world.

My friends encouraged my post about my manuscript by 'liking it' and typing comments. The final response is one worth sharing. *'We have confidence in the Author, you know,'* she said. It warmed my heart to hear it. You and I too can have full confidence in the Author of our lives. He created us. He knows us better than we know ourselves. He permits the rain to fall. Out of those rainy seasons, He will bring a new season of love and beauty, one of gladness and song. Best of all, we have God with us. And we have a hope that will never let us down.

"For I know the plans I have for you,' declares the Lord, 'plans to prosper you and not to harm you, plans to give you hope and a future.' Jeremiah 29:11 NIV

John Wesley, the famous Methodist preacher, was on his death bed. Having lived a life of service to God, he comforted his friends. With difficulty he raised his arm and said with all the strength he could muster: *'The best of all is, God is with us.'* And so today, I reiterate the words spoken by a dying man, a man who lived a victorious life in Jesus. *'The best of all is that God is with us.'*

Lightning Source UK Ltd.
Milton Keynes UK
UKHW01f1002120618
324105UK00009B/467/P